long story short:
from foster care to fame

poems & short stories too big for the stage

bethsheba a. rem

edited by Louis Reyes Rivera and Red Summer

long story short:
from foster care to fame

poems & short stories too big for the stage
bethsheba a. rem

Two Fingers Press Poetry Division 2006
Atlanta, GA

Oya Exclusive International © 2007, 2010, 2011, 2012
Atlanta, GA
Bethsheba A. Rem
www.thequeensheba.org
queensheba811@gmail.com
Facebook: Bethsheba A. Rem & The Queen Sheba

ISBN-10: 097776091X

ISBN-13: 978-0-9777609-1-6

ATTENTION CORPORATIONS, UNIVERSITIES, COLLEGES, AND PROFESSIONAL ORGANIZATIONS: Quantity discounts are available on bulk purchases of this book for educational, gift purposes, or as premiums for increasing magazine subscriptions or renewal. Special books or book excerpts can also be created to fit specific needs. For information, please contact Two Fingers Press, via email at info@twofingerspress.com.

Edited by: Louis Reyes Rivera and Red Summer
Copy Edited by: Stacie Boschma
Original Cover Art: Jaha Zianabu
Book Design: Tiffany Stubbs, Dezign Dogma

delusions of grandeur

long story short:
from foster care to fame

dedication

for, my sun, allerik juwan freeman

I've learned I'm not as good of a communicator as I thought.
I express myself most honestly on the page.
You will not need to read between the lines much here.
There is not a second that goes by that I don't think of you.
Here are the beginnings of my actions.

My only regret: I didn't give you my last name. Maybe you'll
hyphenate it when you turn 18.

You are a miracle and a genius.

May God be your guide; always.

Love,
mom

To everyone whose name I left unchanged, you're welcome.

For those I didn't; you're also welcome.

Dear Mr. Rivera,

You were my first, elder, poetry mentor. You took me on without question. Our first conversation a playful sparing of wits; I liked you immediately. I am grateful you never let me slide or gave me an out. Thank you for walking me through this learning experience over the last five years and pushing me when I wanted to throw the manuscript out the window and let the birds use it for nesting. I enjoyed our discussions on capitalism vs. artist survival; I could feel your smirks when you challenged me to support my claims. The fact that you found intellect in our duals was the main reason I chose to pursue a MFA—I felt confident with you looking over my submission. I know we weren't BFFs but I wish you would have told me...You know I would have yelled back. Scolded you for leaving us in the hands of Hip-Hop. You were a patient teacher. Don't cause trouble up there. Actually—do.

— Sheba

Letter from "my" mother

Aug. 1. 2011

Dear Beth,

It was nice to spend the afternoon with you. I hope your flight home was trouble-free. I bet ███ was glad to see you.

I just want to make sure that you understood me when I said that you must not publish any pictures of anyone but **you** in your book. I noticed that you still took some pictures that had other people in them and if you don't have permission you just can't use them.

I find your writing inflammatory, disturbing and out-right untrue at times and I would not want my picture or anyone else in the family connected with your writing.

A long time ago you gave me some of your slam poetry on CDs. I listened to them in my car on the way home from ███████████ and I was so upset that I came home and wrote you a very lengthy response to what I could only call your venomous diatribe. (Maybe someday I will show you what I wrote.) I thought that by now you would have gotten past that angry stage but I guess not. You gave people your Shebatar CD when you were here in January and someone mentioned how angry you sound—so it isn't just me.

I can't stop you from writing these things – and they are probably a cathartic release for you – but please respect the privacy of others when it comes to their photographs.

Thank you,

███████

Kill all my demons, and my angels might die too.

-Tennessee Williams

the most probable order of things

untitled: haiku #9 11

cardinal 12

civil rights come to pizza hut 17

the woods 21

sun dial 26

untitled: haiku #22 29

junior olympics 30

i's wide shut 35

get it straight 40

clemency 54

most pit: haiku 57

off-beat-i-tis 58

roach motel on central drive 64

the real period poem 70

haiku: for m.i.a. 81

espn: extra special poets network 82

james 88

haiku for john s. blake 100

not exactly the butterfly effect 103

by default 104

the symphony 113

untitled: haiku #23 121

annie 122

normal 128

totally 138

haiku for all wing clippers 145

dear God, it's me sheba 146

my dichotomy 152

the grass isn't always green – er 157

akoben: to the artist 177

untitled: haiku #27 181

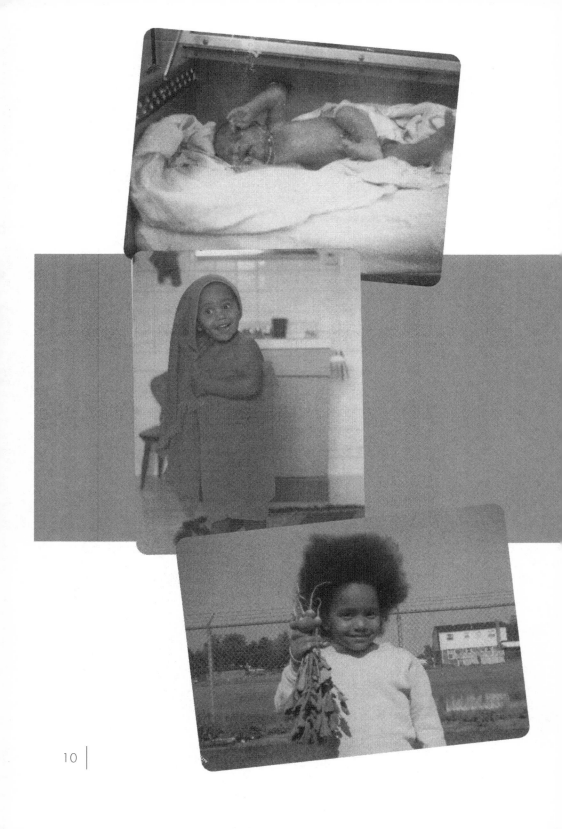

untitled: haiku #9

There are a thousand
poems about you be God.
Believe them; you should

cardinal
dedicated to everyone who moves without apology

A ten year old
walks into my grandmother's closet
a mini
southern Baptist diva,
too young to know
what "Diva" means
struts out;
hat
flopping over her round face.
Wicker bending to kiss her cheek
after each step, a wide
yellow bow trailing down her back
where, one day, she hopes
her wedding dress will be.

One white gloved hand
trying to keep the hat
out of her eyes, to prevent her
from tripping over shoes
flipping off the backs of her heels;
she doesn't care
they're too big
for her to fill;
not an agenda breaker.

The other white-gloved hand
imitating a frantic fanning of the face
as if she was just about to pass out
from heat exhaustion or, from staring at the pastor's
bulge, too long.

Pearls draped
four times around her neck,
red lipstick
smeared from ear to elbow.
One of those Kodak moments

good thing digital wasn't out then;
too many pictures to erase and
forget; eaten up by bad
memory.
First day of fifth grade:
"Does it look like I want my brother's hand-me-downs?!
I am too patent-leather Mary Janes
and Hello Kitty for that!"

My mother dressed us
in the same Save-Mart clothes
the entire neighborhood wore.
I'd always find a phone booth on the way to the bus-stop;
peeled back jackets
she's waiting for me to grow into,
jeans not too trendy not too tight.

At recess we were already practicing hairstylists and
clothing designers;
switching tops and ideas.
Scissors; the original 5-in-1 tool,
turned sweatshirts into mini-skirts
and a completely good pair of tights to fishnets.
Re-combing and twisting each other's hair on the steps
while boys ran in circles chasing dust.

College; my brother's old fatigues turned patchwork
Skirt, afro and Angela Davis t-shirt had folk
clutching their purses
like a running back trying to make first down.
"It's Kinko's people! I'm trying to copy a chap book
for Christ's sake!"
Wanted to get my word out to the people;
let them know the revolution is coming
and me wearing my brother's fatigues 24 days straight
symbolized my quiet protest
until they sent all the troops home.
Wanted my chap book to reveal how them boys were fighting
something they didn't understand or
believe in.

My brother lost his life three days
after they sent him off to war.
He decided his government issued 9-Millimeter
would taste better than cold turkey on rye, that day,
for lunch.
No note, no nothin'!
Just a few orderlies to clean up his remains.
Chunks of brain tissue caught
between the fibers of the mop and sponge
smearing him into the wood grain on the mess hall floor.
Brings new meaning to drift wood.

On Vacation;
my white parents
tried their best
to play color match
with their negro child.
They were hippies
flower children,
caught between: The Movement and privilege.
Adopting me, they said,
was their effort to try and save the world.
"Vengeance is mine"
said the Lord.
Lucky for them their color
would fade.

Humans run in packs
or herds
Fine,
I'm head high,
in front
with the family in tow;
leading but careful not to let my
10-year-old strut
separate me
completely.
Forgive me for not sounding, looking like you
expect me to.

There are two types of people in the world:
me and
everybody else.

'Awesome thing is: you can repeat the same mantra;
find you a compact, a
rearview or dark windows on a building as you're
speed-walking through lunch,
repeat three times daily and call on me
never.
This is the part where I should give you all the reasons why;
naw, we're past all that.
If you don't know, we won't feel sorry
for you; 'cause we won't even know you're
alive.

This is how it's always going to be:
I'm always going left
when the world says North,
I'm wearing plaid and polka-dots when solids are in;
my cadence will always be rocker
meets Hip-Hop; before life support.
I'm not down for making up misery when
I'm having a good day and I will always
want to slit my wrists after a horrific break-up
but I won't
'cause I'm too fly and that's it,
simple.

Awesome thing is there is room on the block for
all us geniuses

This poem is about us
and how it seems to be a Cardinal sin for us to think we're
great; well,
I happen to look up Cardinal:
N. *much sought-after cage birds highly valued for their*
song and color

You know the new saying: We are known by the pastors
we keep.

Listen, you live 80 years to be dead for, like, ever.

Look, life is like masturbation; do you!

Trick is:
not to think
you're better and never believe
you're worse.

Go.

civil rights comes to pizza hut

Pizza Hut. Of all places. It wasn't like it was some fancy French restaurant in the 'burbs that would be totally oblivious to any situation like this.

Pizza Hut? I couldn't believe we were at Pizza Hut for this information anyway. This kind of family gathering should have happened at a restaurant where after you left a tip the waiter could fill up his gas tank. Pizza it was.

The other thing that killed me was that there wasn't anyone else standing there waiting to be seated. So how could that bitch not have noticed that we were to-ge-ther? There were six of us including my older brother's girlfriend who became a permanent member of our family after their second year of dating.

I hated her. I hated all of them.

Almost 13 years of waiting to be recognized, 13 years of waiting to belong, 13 years of waiting to be acknowledged as a selected individual, not an addition to be molded. I was still waiting. I was pissed off constantly and was looking for any opportunity for an outburst, so here was my small moment of glory.

It couldn't have been much later than six o'clock. My father routinely got home from work around four thirty and I got home from track practice around 5:15 p.m. When a school bus driver saw me running in three feet of mid-winter Michigan snow to catch the last ride to school, he quickly suggested I join his city-wide track team to relieve some of my cultural frustrations on the track, not on my ethnically challenged family.

I remember changing my clothes quickly because my mother informed me, on the way in the door, that we were going out for dinner. I ran upstairs to clean up and smooth some lotion over my bronze skin that turned ash in the shower. I fumbled with the brush as I smoothed back my bushy black hair into a long braid that hung past my shoulders.

I wasn't allowed to get a relaxer until I turned 16. My mother learned from our next-door neighbor that relaxers tend to fry virgin hair if applied too young. I had two years to go. I hurried downstairs and my mother was tying up her stringy brown hair she inherited from the German side of her family. Not that our family couldn't afford it, but my mother cooked seven days a week and going to dinner was definitely considered a treat.

So we get there. Pizza Hut. Around 6:00 p.m. I'm in an even mood. Not up or down but always anticipating. I remember it being bright outside and all of Pizza Hut was lit up. It had to be summer. In the North it stays light out late in the summer and I don't remember wearing a coat. I hate wearing a coat, so I would have remembered.

Longer than we should have, but not long enough for my father to say anything, was how long we waited until the $2.12-makin' — thinkin' she has control over how long we waited for her two bit half-assed greeting — bitch, came up and said what would have been fatal words for her if my so-called family wasn't standing there.

My father at the time was six feet two inches tall and at least 235 pounds. He had thinning salt and pepper hair he swooped to one side of his head. He was going through the mid-life "I am not really balding" denial period. Despite the shiny spot that was first to sunburn in the summer he was a man of stature. What he said, I respected, followed, but not always agreed with. Like this. There were hardly any other customers in the restaurant. I guess it being Monday, pizza, after junk food weekend, was not high on everyone's list for dinner.

The chick walked up like she desperately needed some help with the one other table that came for fine dining this evening, and grabbed some menus out of the wooden holder.

Her strides were short and fast. It looked as if she were trying not to break out in a small gallop. It was the middle of summer and when she took her forearm to wipe the sweat off her brow I noticed her palm and forehead were the same color. Her chalky skin made me realize she looked like she had been locked in a closet for a year. Her bleached blond ponytail was filthy with grease and it stuck together as it bounced back and forth in the rubber band that was holding it behind her head.

Now I was leaning. I thought we had waited too long and I was anxious to hear this "news" my father had called this oh-so-important meeting for. My father's torso was directly in front of me, lucky for the bitch. I don't remember who was standing next to me, but it didn't matter.

Her pale face flushed red over her freckles, and almost out of breath, the bitch glanced over our group and said, "How many? Five?" That registered to my always looking for an excuse to blow up at racism brain. At that moment, 13 years of repressed anger for situations like this gone unnoticed flashed across my inner eye like an eclipse. I couldn't take it anymore. I refused to be invisible in a world I obviously was destined to contribute so much to. They chose me to be a part of their family 13 years ago, and it had taken this very moment for me to arrive.

"Five?" I was literally yelling.

My whole family turned to glare at me. I kept going. I didn't care. Still don't. Erect now and trying to push past my father who knew exactly what was going on. "Five?" (I repeated again.) "You see me standing here! What are you trying to say? Try SIX lady!"

I tried really hard not to swear even though my father cursed worse than a sailor did in normal conversation. "Shut up Beth," my father yelled. They called me Beth then. I could tell my mother was embarrassed. My older brother and his airhead blond bimbo walked off like they didn't know us.

I do remember that two bit-$2.12 makin, wanna' work in a real restaurant, server, mumbling an apology and correcting herself. It was too late. My mood went from level to escalated in those brief milliseconds and I didn't care. Glad I am sure.

Tension, of course, was the appetizer for our pizza and the next very long hour and half. My father told us that his father, who recently passed, had left a will. "Oh, God," I thought. We could have made pizza for this. That was the cause of our outing, a will. After all that, I wasn't even in the damn thing. Once again included in separation. They could have left me at home. I had homework anyway.

I knew that each day my, selected, family prayed I was content and would stay level. Never knowing when I was going to blow. My family couldn't understand that in my situation, it was very hard to let anything that seemed discriminating fly.

It got to be too much for me the next year or so. I left on my birthday the following summer and promised myself that, even if people were confused for those 15 years, the rest of my life, I would make my position clear.

the woods

"Let's get lost!"
my father would yell from the driver's seat.

Mini-Vans were a new trend.
My older brother and I were, only, divided
by the cooler filled with juice boxes
home made cookies
and Rice Crispy treats.
We'd relax behind the invisible
wall that separated us from our
parents
trying to out stare each other
in silence;
if we only knew, then,
calculated speech
holds more depth,
has more power.

Mother would smile
at our father's announcement
adjust her seatbelt
preparing for the ride.
It's not that he didn't want to know
where he was going,
he didn't ask for
directions because he was a 6'2" 250 lbs
intimidating stature of a man or
his early salt and pepper beard
hid too much pride
covering a smile
and twinkling eyes
like a Cheshire at night.
No, he didn't ask for directions
he said, because strangers don't know
the path you've taken
or from whence you've come
so, how would they be able
to point you in the right direction?

Vultures have eaten
your berry path
leading back to safety
bears have clawed away
your yellow ribbon
on the old oak tree
you will have to tread
the current
fight
the stream
up hill
to rid your scent
from the blood hounds
attached to rifles.
Getting lost,
my father would say,
is just a way
of finding your way out.

Rolling through the back roads
my father instructed us
to close our eyes
and throw up our hands
like we were in a roller coaster.
Just because you have an idea,
he would shout
over the enthusiastic wind
of the open window,
Just because you have an idea
doesn't mean it belongs to you.

Learn to let go
and things will come easily

I am lost
I don't want to be here
I have left myself
no way out
no trap door

no secret wall panels
no loop holes
or escape clauses

Decisions aren't hard
he'd say at a crossroad
my mother shaking her head
they can be painful
there's a difference
Reload
Rewind
Fill up before the bridge-tunnel
Pull the weeds

If you happen
to get into a fender bender
with a deer,
duck;
my father warned,
stern and unwavering.
The buck will kick to survive
withstand glass and metal
to hunt tomorrow.

Exit your vehicles
leave what you know to be safe;
live to sift through the wreckage.
This is not Paramount
there will be no music
before the explosion.

Right as my brother
began to cross
the imaginary divide
of the snack cooler to annoy me,
just as my mother's patience couldn't pretend to
flip through one more
magazine page, that
magic moment

exactly before my eyes
grew tired of squinting by the dome light and the
yellow lines rushing by our tires
were about to make me nauseous -
the trees parted
gravel gave way to pavement and
all the wild animals
halted at the dam.

My father could feel
restlessness
through the back of his seat
If he said "youngin'"
he didn't have to look at either one of us
we knew who he was addressing.
"Careful of that short fuse, youngin';
you're likely to burn your bridges."

It is not fair
that you think you love me
I am not sure
you are wrong for it
I am a lot of work
you are a lot of excuses.
It's no coincidence
that the position to rest
and the position to pray
are the same.

It took me a few summers
to realize my father
had this route memorized
kept the directions
on the flip side of his sun visor.

Years later,
I inquired about his
tolerance;
my brother and I quarreling

in the backseat,
our mother's supposed aggravation at the
extended route
through the woods.

Why didn't he just give in?
Take the short cut
we all knew he knew?

There was that Cheshire grin, again
"Life," I could hear the acoustics off his chin
as he started rustling his fingers
through his Brillo sponge of a beard

"Life is only a competition
if you have something to lose."

sun dial
sonnet for my sun, Allerik

Remember your Gods; Nike and Aramid
call on them when the voices are too loud
Find a corner. Raise your hands. Kneel and pray.
Summons the discipline of your mother
the muscle of your father and relax.
Speak directly in the ear of your Lord
and confess your premeditated blunders.
The women will be tempting; O' I know.
Sweets and sugars will be offered on plates of gold.
Careful they are not laced with lye
or hallucinogens. Jealousy owns
a vast wardrobe. Buttons will be shiny.
When a stranger appears offering ad-
vice, ask them to first remove their fur coat.

You know who you are

untitled: haiku #22

Therapy makes me angry
I paid a stranger for my
grand-mama's advice

junior olympics

The smell of freshly baked chocolate chip cookies, from scratch, lingered in the air. I bounced down the steps, two at a time, in my homemade pink pajamas with fuzzy feet. I knew about logos at an early age; this one had a rabbit on it.

Father would joke and say, "You made boy and girl cookies because some of them have nuts."

You laughed while placing them, proportionately, in three brown paper bags my older brother, Kevin, father and I would depart with the next morning.

My cookies never made it to school. Either eaten on the way or traded for some chocolate-peanut butter combination I still crave during certain times of the month and on other special occasions.

It was the end of a two-week Christmas break; I was anxious to get back to school. I hated being home. It was boring. There are only so many things you can do with snow and you made me do stupid stuff, like read. And then I had to tell you what the book was about, like you didn't know.

"You're the one that brought it from the library! You read it!"

This yelling, of course, was going on all in my head. I knew better. I was taller than you even then, but, father, whoa(!), I digress; to keep me and my overactive brain busy, you would challenge me to memorize state capitals and practice long division. Your way to get me to do it? Say I couldn't.

Irony. Still seems to work, today.

I despised you.

I wanted to go to the mall with the other 12-year-olds with no money. You said there was no point in going if I didn't have any money. It would only provoke me to steal. "If you lie —

you steal; if you steal – you'd kill," you'd chant in a nursery rhyme tone disguised as a social warning.

Most of my time was spent dressing up, from head to toe, in the clothes I got for Christmas, and standing at our window for hours, watching cars splash mud on passersby.

By the end of the first week, I couldn't take it anymore. You asked far too much of me. Really? Take out the trash with He-Man coming on in two minutes!? So I pretended to take the trash out because I'm 12, and I can outsmart you. I decided to leave it on the side of the house and run away, thinking this would solve everything!

I sprinted down the block, vowing never to come back to this horrific household of chores, responsibilities and learning! It was obscene to ask a pre-teen to think during vacation. How could you? I stood at the end of the block, fuming – plotting all the ways I'd make you pay and suffer for your cruelty.

Just as I was ready to make a mad dash to freedom and take on the world at 12, an overwhelming sensation took over my body. Ice.

I had forgotten my coat.

Realizing this was a lose-lose situation and He-Man was probably half over, I pried my frozen Asics from the ground and returned to you, sipping from a mug of hot chocolate and holding a belt. It didn't dawn on me until later that your hour-long speech about how big and ferocious Detroit is, how 12-year-olds should never be alone – and where was I going anyway? – was just your ploy to let my buns thaw out; stalling until father got home. Key in the door and you suddenly grew weary of preaching.

Nice move, mom.

The minute he walked in, you handed the belt to him and gave him the speed-reader version of my great escape from the trash.

As if the belt had magic powers; his exhaustion from work recharged the longer he gripped the rawhide; the buckle lit up and sparks flew everywhere as it whizzed through the air. Like a ballerina coming down from heroine, I leapt and spun to avoid the blows.

II

Over those next few years, making the city track team was a mistake that turned into a healthy outlet for my anger.

There was that blinding winter morning when the rising sun bounced sunbeams off the ice and snow, and then it pulled back again as if it didn't want to get out of bed at 6:00 a.m. either. It was one of those days when everything's late. One of those mornings when you start late, end late, and everything in between is running behind the exact amount of time you left on the snooze button; every time the alarm went off, more minutes were added to the procrastination. Formula for a stressful day: calculate how much longer you could sleep than time you had left.

Still getting dressed in the car, the steam increase from the exhaust pipe on the yellow bellied school bus, now turned industrial grey from Detroit's morning rush-hour smog, slowly scraping the ground meant 7:15 a.m. was here and I wasn't. The car didn't come to a complete stop before I flung open the door to the house-size Caprice Classic Grandmother gave us after the 1976, sea-green, Nova had broken down the month before.

The warmth of your breath etched the words, "Have a great day at school," in icicle letters that seemed to shatter and disappear into thin air as the door slammed behind me. Now, wide awake, I was hurdling three-foot snow caps effortlessly, gallop broke to stride, back-pack bouncing to the rhythm of each connection, heel to pavement, lungs filled with frozen needles, I yelled, "Wait!" with my blue mitten in the air waving snowflakes from my sight path.

The school bus doors flung open, and a substitute driver was grinning harder than that disappearing Cheshire cat; he hands me a business card out of thin air. "Have your parents call me," he said.

That night, I sat at the table, knee bouncing like a jackhammer awaiting the outcome of this business card business. Father was on the phone talking to the substitute bus driver with less expression than his Friday night poker game face.
It was hard to determine the content of his, "…Uh-huh, uh-huh, uuuh-huuuhs…" He hung up the phone and gave me the news.

Track?! At 12?!

What is it with this trying to keep me healthy and fit and active thing? Another ploy to harness my energy; they were scheming again. The only running I wanted to do was behind 8th grade boys.

III

Sixteen years later, dust rarely hits the row of medals I keep by my bedside in chronological order of wins. There's a gap between Junior Olympics '91 and '92. I pinned it on father's shirt in '97. It was my first trip home since '86. I thought he might be able to show it to God when he got there. Since Heaven has always been taught as a place of bliss, I've always believed no one would recognize anyone when granted admittance to keep away the pain of memories.

Father cried in the hospital a few days before he passed. I told him I thought he was always so hard on me because he loved his boys more. Tears made chalky lanes down his sunken cheeks in the plaster the cancer was turning his skin to; I'd never seen this vulnerability in his overwhelming frame before. He said he was always so hard on me because he didn't want me to turn out like his boys. He pushed me because he was proud of me.

I stopped racing in 1992, when I graduated high school. Now we're divorced, if we can be divorced. You sent me a card for my birthday. I got it late. I didn't even read it. Ripped it open for money and used the lousy $20 for gas and a bottle of water.

I only make cookies from frozen batter, and the only things I sew are rips along the seams and buttons on old jackets. Now I write for a living and for anger management, and I've taken to practicing math problems while keeping slam scores.

Recently, God stripped me of several things I thought meant something to me. Just the other day, I decided to take up racing again; rekindle my relationship with 6 a.m.; feel weightless against the ground; let the wind cut through my lungs in the mornings as I'd whiz past on-lookers. Countless numbers of city blocks swooshing by in a blur while my mind is distracted by my list of things to do.

We don't have Michigan winters in Virginia, but sometimes, right in the middle of winter, it gets cold enough for mittens.

i's wide shut

Protective
I don't crack jokes in public
I am afraid someone will see us laughing
enjoying each other's company
in misery.

This was supposed to be beautiful
slumber parties
pedicures and
beauty secrets.

Coming out
to friends and family is nothing
like the fear
of reject military personnel demoted to police officers
that take pride in ripping flesh from bone;
Billy club crushing eardrum,
blood ruining a sunny day
and a fifth date.
Embarrassed like a girl's introduction to womanhood
in the middle of gym class
we are still unprepared;
shocked, even.
Covering our wounds with our hands
more to keep in our pride and to mute
out the taunting laughter;
our fingers too small to hold back
blood
pushing through like a geyser.

Each repeat beating
she became the target because,
"she thinks she's a boy",
they managed to say between breaths.
Sweat soaking their uniforms,
clinging to strands of hair like suicide jumpers

not ready to make a final decision,
fists firing like the finale in a holiday sky
her body flopping back and forth
spin-cycle on the concrete.
"Take it like a man!"
Her ribs crack
Jolted my arm out of socket
ripped away from the two uniforms
it took to hold me back, flung my stomach
and breasts over her head,
wrapped my arms around
her sides, they grab a stray branch
from a nearby watching tree,
pipe from a stolen car;
my arm breaks.

Tread marks on my back
I thought of two rap songs
9-1-1 is a joke in your town.

28% of officers do not assist or adequately report
hate crimes concerning the gay and lesbian community

1964
civil?
Right.
The left wing couldn't fly yet
had feathers missing
I know movies aren't the best
source of reference
I cried through Brokeback Mountain.
She and I are neither:
white
nor privileged.
And if two white men in America
don't feel free and safe
well,
we are not covered either;
not by doctrine
nor by health care.

II

Lunch on campus;
we don't share dessert like at home.
We keep our puddings separate.
Against her insistence I won't allow
her to carry my books
or open my doors;
my eyes follow my shoelaces when we pass in the breezeway.
This was supposed to be simpler:
built in HOV and fashion consultant,
in vitro fertilization
or adoption.

Pet names stopped sophomore year
We'd meet each other
in the community garden
my nose grazed her cheek
lips brushed against each others' quickly
eyes darting around to check for spies
that fawn look of *"I miss you too"*
Giggling we'd rush off like kindergarten recess.

III

On date night
we'd role play strangers at the bar

Tonight, the light above the ATM was out
the alley, familiar graffiti
and condoms from truant high school
scholars
still pumped from:
wrestling practice
and illegal steroids;
it took eight of them to pin me down.

I was a virgin.

Wire hangers
bottles
broken glass
finally, the courage
of themselves.
Swollen salty tongues muffled
my attempt to put after school special lessons
to use.
Yelling "EARTHQUAKE!"
wouldn't have worked
People must be numb
to "FIRE!"
like I am numb
to hope.

"You just need a man to help change your mind"

Thank you for helping me.
Chewing half a tongue
like cud, my only evidence,
he was screaming.
Blood dripped between my teeth
Lestat became my hero
Crack! my jaw broke
My high cheek bones
effortlessly became gravel
beneath their knuckles
knocked loose
like a child wiping out on his Schwinn on a dirt road;
knees in my stomach and throat.

According to the US Department of Justice,
somewhere in America,
a woman is raped every two minutes;

Picking up our love
after:
the gurney
the siren

after:
the metal clamps
bright lights and cold emergency room

after:
the athletes
protected by scholarship and alumni

after:
the bench and the gavel
after:
prosecution team vs. public defender
the reporters and
predetermined verdict in the headlines

after:
sleeping in separate beds,
separate rooms
not sleeping

Picking up the innocence
in our romance
was like picking up a fallen mirror
broken in its frame:

If you lose one piece
you could ruin the entire thing

If you are careful, over time,
love can be
restored.

get it straight
inspired by real life events

You know how you're having an argument,
you can't come up with a quick enough come back;
then, in the middle of the night
the perfect retaliation hits you like you're in a V-8 ad?

You roll over and try to give your new-found reply
as much conviction as you had four hours ago
but after the make-up sex
you kinda' lose some steam?
your answer comes out of left Field of Dreams
and ends up falling, well, just falling?
This is kinda' like that, not really, kinda-sorta.

First thing:
I'm not a lesbian

Second thing:
I'm not a lesbian

Third thing:
I'm not a lesbian

I'm never going to be a lesbian
I don't claim lesbian on my taxes
I don't try and get double the discounts when offered
for minorities

I'm not a lesbian in training
part time
full time
half time
double time
prime time
central standard time
CP time

I'm not pretending
to be a lesbian
I don't play one
on late night cable
pornos
or YouTube
maybe on MySpace
if the sponsorship is right
No, no – I take that back
not *even* if the sponsorship was right
it's never right.

I am not a lesbian

I'm not rockin' rainbows
or triangles
or pride t-shirts
multi-colored thongs
or rearview mirror ornamentation that says:
come break into my car
because my life is carefree
full of:
fun, expensive trips,
shopping sprees
and day spas
while you
heterosexual tight-asses
have to go home to:
a cow of a wife
kids you're not sure are yours
and dust-mites.

I am not a lesbian

I don't have gay friends
I don't buy gay furniture
I don't buy gay clothes
I don't listen to gay music

Oh – we all know what "gay music" is!
We can all be standing around
quietly socializing
and as soon as some *gay music* comes on
every extra gay person
is immediately on blast
completely given away, Vogue-ing
down the isles of Tar-jay
'cause someone at the customer service counter
was feeling a tad overwhelmed with the long
holiday lines and decided to pump up the
Musak on the overhead speakers. If one out of four
people are gay, an average of 12 people just started
twisting their arms over their heads
spinning on the toes of their shell toes and
doing the bounce-split down the kitchen isle.

But, I am not a lesbian
so I am immune
to this "gay music"
and I can listen to it
full stereo – unmoved

My bank account
is usually on E
negative E
E minus
so, I don't even *qualify*
to be a lesbian
Third thing, part F
<u>she</u> cornered *me* in the bathroom

she already knew her answer
just wanted to "check".
Wanted to validate
if what she heard was "true".
"I asked somebody, earlier, if you were gay," She says.

Tab out – first problem, sister,
you asked someone else – Tab in

Now, my lipstick was crooked.
Fuming, I say, extra sexy just to fuck with her,
"Awesome; what'd they say?"
"They said 'yeah Sheba's gay, I thought everyone knew.'"
Uh, clearly not, 'cause I didn't know.
That part was in my head.
 This part was out loud:
"Really, well, tell them to come hollah at me
and we'll see how much of a lesbian I really am."
Which I know,
I know!
I-already-know
was a whack-ass answer, but that's all
I could fucking think of
at the time,
which is the whole reason
for this rant
in the first place.

There must have been a glitch
in the Matrix
the next part
was definitely out loud:
"Are you straight?" she smacks the question
on the counter
along with all the other dirt,
grime and pubic hairs
in this public bathroom.

"Yup," I said, slowly rubbing my lip-gloss together
and staring dead in her eyes like they teach you
in The Secret.

Shit, ass, fuck, damn, motha-fuckin-bean sucker, Astroturf
builder, fuck-ass, bastard of a saber-toothed giraffe with fleas.
That part was in my head.

She left, wah-wah'-ing
some shit about liking my poetry.

Bitch, fuck you, I just feel raped.

You took with you
the one thing
we spend our lives building:
Identity
You just said fuck it, Im'ma label you
what I want and tell everyone else
like it's the truth.

Bush doesn't like Black people; try that rumor instead.

Fuckin' bitch I hate her guts.

If one more person
asks me if I'm gay,
I'm going to beat the breaks off of them.
No questions
No flinching
No hesitating
right across the nose
and upper teeth.
Talk shit no more.

You know what's gay?
People who stand around
and discuss who's gay;
that's gay.

Get a life.
Better yet:
play in traffic.

Be concerned
about anything, other than what the fuck I'm doing.
Don't-ask-me-no-questions-and-I-won't-tell-you-no-lies.
When you see me with multiple women
they may just happen to be...my friends!
Geezus.

Don't ask me shit

Ever heard of Don't ask, Don't tell?
Oh, that's only applicable to all the solders we send off to kill?

You eat pussy
every time you kiss and
let him back in.
He won't answer where he's been; wrinkled Oxford
missing buttons on his collar
creases in the lap of his jeans
come on!
No, you can't watch
No, you can't tape it
No you can't bring a friend
if you and your friend have time
to take out of your day, to drive
half way across town
set up a camera
camera phone
web cam
iPhone (4)
to sit and watch
two women
for, say, six to 10 hours
when you're only used to hmmmmmm
six-to-10 minutes,
engage in something inconceivable
to your primitive
thinking
if you have time
like that, then it's no wonder
why you're:
broke, single and desperate.
Maybe now,
that the "government" has captured 40 million
phone numbers for National Security
you'll be able
to get a date

You can even thank baby Bush for the pick up line:
"Girl you need to give me yo' number, I'm tryin' to keep you
safe, you know we in code orange and shit, it's a matter of
national security, so give me yo' number so I can check on
you..."

And if your loser-ass
happens to be in a relationship
you're probably fucking miserable, 'cause most people believe
love is crafted
not chemistry

Trust - I don't ever
want to watch
you and your girlfriend fuckin'.
I am not interested
in seeing either one of you
naked
at-all.
Ever.
If I wanted to fuck
your girlfriend
I would have;
however, hygiene is important, to me and most of you
nasty motha-fuqua's
are so dirty
you look...greasy;
like you ain't seen a bath;
like you didn't know porcelain
had made it past customs, yet.
A fucking walking dust ball.
You stank
your breath stinks
you look nasty...
do you look in the mirror
and think
that's attractive?

1 - You clearly don't have any friends and

2 - Kill yourself

No -
it won't rub off
it's not contagious
unless, of course, you're susceptible to
happiness
which, judging by your cheap shoes, crusty
lipstick and crows feet
the only thing you attract
is misery.

I understand it may not be a part of your culture;
you're, clearly, not part of ours.

You're ugly
and your mother dresses you funny.
Oh-Yeah, Oh-Yeah, I talked about yo mama!
'cause every time you disrespect me
you're talkin' about mine.
you think maybe my mama
didn't spend enough time with me,
maybe she fell short of her responsibilities
maybe she should have taught me about
the birds and the bees?

Tab out – (which by the way are two different species and
could never really get together anyway, kinda' like the giraffe,
in the children's cold medicine commercial that has two
warthogs for children, whoever let that commercial through
marketing should be fired, you are confusing children! Don't
give me that "Maybe they were adopted" shit. Giraffes can't
fill out the paper work and there is a 5-year waiting period on
warthog adoption in this country) – Tab in
you think, maybe,
she could have talked me out of it
told me it's wrong

to love someone that looks like me?
Rewind:
1979
back seat of the family car
on the way home
from some family function
I've since forgotten,
my mother held the scarlet letter
in her hand;
a four-page explanation
why my father's sister's lover, Bonnie,
decided to start a medical procedure at
The University of Michigan
that would, ultimately, make her
a man

We were to immediately start calling Bonnie, Matt.
Matt had to conduct himself like a man
for two years
before U of M would consent
to surgery.

She had to prove she was man enough.

I think we lose our genius with our virginity.

Five-years-old I asked my mother;
"Since Bonnie wouldn't have had the surgery yet, wouldn't that
just make her
woman enough?"

Kicking the back of my father's seat,
I started crying
and scolding
and asking a million questions.
Neither of my parents raised their voices;
calmly explained why this was so important:
Matt would have to use men's bathrooms
clothing

change her hair
use barbershops
instead of beauty salons
walk-ins instead of appointments
stop asking for directions when she was lost,
sit and walk differently,
totally lose
who she was
to become
who she wants;
more importantly
believes
she should be.

If only we were all so brave.

She said the locker rooms at the gym
were the worst
hiding her body was no problem
cupped in the palm of her hands
bent over between her knees on the bathroom floor
fetal position,
like she was trying to undo
what was already done
she said, she still couldn't hide her ears.

We all rumor
about what is said
behind the oily mist and salty sweat
of a men's club
or a barbershop, mid-day
before the mothers bring their sons
after school for tapers and Caesars
We couldn't imagine the discussions, she said.

Matt said she felt like a man
her whole life
it ate at her
until she decided

to make a change
when most people can't
face themselves

she said she didn't want to discuss
private sector gossip, with me
men are beautiful people;
Some day
one will whisk me off my feet
and take me to Dairy Queen
I guess, that's how she conveyed marriage
to a 5-year-old; Dairy Queen.
And I believed her
and everyone else
Until I, just, didn't,
anymore.

Present Day:
Two is the loneliest number.

Your theory:
spend eight seasons dating
one Valentine's Day (eve) breaking-up
seven years engaged
three phony Easter Sunday dinners
in an itchy dress
[neither one of us is Catholic]
six years living together
trying to figure out how to leave
four months married
hate my spouse after three
one night with a stripper
and the next 8 months and $1400 dollars
on a personal trainer after
eating my way out of depression

Tab – that's what she said – End Tab

People stay together for lower

car insurance payments
these days.
Love is never the first thing
out of anyone's mouth
or manners
Love went out of style in the 80s with Polyester
and the Bushes
but we keep bringing them back.

We're going to beat ourselves into submission

We master moving
through the house
not touching
each other
sleeping
on a 4 x 6 box of feathers
and hardship
not touching
each other
share the same mirror
bathroom and closet space
and never touch
each other
then wonder why
we can never make
the connection

Two times like double-dutch
treading lightly while trying not to trip.

Urban legend says: It comes
when you're not looking for it
or when you sober up;
either way, I had on cheap sunglasses.

Tooth and nail
boxing gloves and Jello
I fought it;

didn't want labels
landing on me like sticky notes
released from a GoodYear blimp.

But, if love is:
warming up my heating pad for my knees
and cramps
sharing favorite foods and TV shows
pretending to share
favorite foods and TV shows
a glass of wine on our deck and a foot rub
If love is sacrificing living comforts
to encourage each others dreams
then this ain't about gender.

Your theory;
I shouldn't love
someone that allows me to eat peanut butter and honey
off a spoon 'cause I'm a bread-a-phobe slash sugar-a-holic.

I'm not a lesbian;
I have loved women,
just like I have loved men
and I think, I'd rather love
someone who allows me my own honey jar
than someone
who has to come behind me
and catch me double dipping
While we're sharing blankets
and memories
you'll still be fighting
still be star-69n'
catching your man skeet-skeetin all over your keyboard
in chat-rooms and on iChat with your new neighbor
during your next 'Baby-Mama makes peace with the Chicken
Heads' meeting
during the next midnight drawing of the straws
to see which of you lames are carrying

Meth in your twat
through the metal detectors and over the county line;
think of me.

Go back to the bathroom
rewind your feeble excuse of a life
back to the part you took my identity
and decided it belonged to someone
other than me

Think of me; think of me, I say
sex on the beach in one hand and
sex on the beach in the other, you know…

Hear me clearly when I tell you,
'cause this part is OUT loud:
I'm straight, {shawty.}
The question is:
Are you?

clemency

Losing a child
is like being front row at the execution of your favorite lover,

your nose, breath and tears pressed behind the glass,
you're side-eyeing the guard and his gun—

stoic chalky faces, blue suits, shirts with too much starch—
—the single silver knob on the only door—

and you're praying the red phone hanging on the wall
next to the priest, will ring.

Love is an Action

most pit: haiku

Sonic hamburger
cheesy fries and Listerine;
results of resin

offbeatitis
[awf-beet-eye-tis]
-noun; infectious disease. Susceptible, only, to those
that create their own way

Have you ever become off beat while watching someone else dance?

Or

It's that part of the concert when all the instruments in the band fall out, except the drums; the entire audience is rocking simultaneously and suddenly you realize you're clapping and singing at the same time and immediately become off beat?

Or

You're in the car with several close friends and it happens. You can feel your heart beat start to increase inside your shirt. The air-conditioning is on full blast but your forehead begins to bead. You know what's about to happen. The most popular song in the entire world comes on the radio and all your friends motivate to sing along, effortlessly. You thought you were prepared. You downloaded this song on your MP3 player and practiced the lyrics and memorized the music for the last week or so. It starts to play and your friends, as if rehearsed, ask you to turn it up.

You're feeling confident and join the passenger choir now reaching full octave and volume. You start to bob your head, careful to count the bars you've studied in the private of your bathroom concerts; a smile pushes the corners of your mouth and you jump right in, landing perfectly on the right words, flawlessly in tune with your ultra cool friends, whom you secretly envy in their ability to pick up and adapt to music like recycled fashion.

Your certainty is through the moon-roof! You even take the right hand off the wheel, leaving the very secure position of 10 and two and start to pump your fist in the air and over exaggerate your head nods (making sure not to lose count), imitating the latest rock video you've studied on YouTube.

Then it happens. The radio is playing the remix. You haven't studied the remix! The beat suddenly changes and although the computation is still the same, void of digitized sound and drum machines, you fall straight off your high. The cliff of cool you've built in the last five minutes with your friends has just crumbled. You're singing loud and wrong while your best friends, since the Big Wheel raced down your driveway, are covering their mouths with their engagement ring hands pretending to cough. You realize you have completely lost the song and cool points.

It's not your fault; you *may* have Offbeatitis.

This "disease" is brought on when one is so overcome with excitement and pure joy of performance that they suddenly become oblivious to all instruments created to keep time and rhythm and their body starts moving at an "incorrect" pace or speed, thus causing the performance to lose meter and *appear* as if the patient is "off beat".

It is important to note that this patient will appear completely capable of such activities especially during a low-to-no pressure situation such as practice or rehearsal times and/or spaces. Their rhythm will be completely intact, dance moves thoroughly comprehensible and they will have complete control over all their bodily functions.

However, when the lights go up, the audience is glaring at the said patient and the musical instruments specifically called upon and set in place to assist such artist...errr, patient, begin to cohesively manipulate sound in a collective manner, such patient will (clearly) step outside of themselves and let the evil spirit of the Offbeatitis infection consume their bodies.

It is important to not touch, interrupt, lean towards, make any sudden moves (this will confuse the patient even more) or loud noises in the direction of the patient. Do *not* approach the patient!

Unfortunately, if there happens to be an early onset of Offbeatitis at the beginning of any musical performance, it will *not* automatically disappear when the current song/number/ performance is over. Although, this dreadful disease can appear pretty abruptly, it leaves the blood stream gradually only after the body and brain recognize that the <u>entire</u> performance has subsided. It may be several minutes or hours before Offbeatitis is completely out of the system.

The FDA is not completely familiarized with this new disease; an official statement has not been released, yet, to clarify if Offbeatitis affects the brain only or the blood and brain. So far, it seems to manipulate both.

First, Offbeatitis is recognized by receptors in the brain that translate the music, sound and rhythm backwards, sometimes upside down, in some serious cases (Ukrane Ludicris Concert 2004) sideways! It may, instantaneously, interpret what the brain is hearing as inaccurate or in the incorrect order and attempts to correct the malfunctioning signal by moving in the off number.

For instance if the said instigators (instruments and other rhythm machinery) are in a harmony in 2-4 time, the brain interprets this as 4-2 and truly believes that if it begins the body's movement in a 1-3, thusly a 3-1 movement ensues.

We believe Offbeatitis also infects the blood flow. If you notice the patient beginning to sweat while all other subjects within the same area and on the perimeter are calm and, in fact, wondering why the patient is soaking through their clothes. If the, obviously, uninfected group begins eyeing each other in sideways glances as not to distract or disturb the patient; take note and begin running, as fast as you can, to a wide open area as to not become trapped; you are witnessing the infiltration of Offbeatitis into the bloodstream. This may cause heatstroke, overeating, rashes, rosacea, coughing, wheezing, addiction to gambling, fear of dogs, heart attack, sudden pregnancy and death.

Fortunately, Offbeatitis is *not* contagious but *does* seem to be passed down generation to generation. It is not even kind enough to skip generations, like twins. The FDA is working on a way to cure Offbeatitis but no such luck, kiddo.

Without a cure, Offbeatitis can cause: families to fall apart, poverty, starvation (Due to constant practicing; the patient believes Offbeatitis can be overcome with memorized repetition to certain basic beats. If the patient is multi-cultural or travels a lot this may become a larger problem.) or immobilization from fear of moving at all.

This disease does transfer to normal and/or daily activity. It is feared a sudden break out may occur if the patient happens upon a high energy area containing the natural reactor: music. The patient must be watched at all times and not allowed to wander into high musically influenced areas where there may be dancing, drum circles or any sort of rhythmic movement by a mass of people, larger than the number - one.

If Offbeatitis patients are not closely monitored their erratic behavior could be misdiagnosed by the untrained eye as a seizure and they can be given the wrong medical treatment.

However, as said earlier, if there are no evident "pressures" such as people who may know the patient, said patient could actually repress the triggers to the brain, thus preventing Offbeatitis toxins from being released into the bloodstream, and become completely happy at just being surrounded by "music" and involuntarily fall into the socially acceptable body movements that mimic and ultimately compliment the beat.

If *you* have, or *know* someone who has Offbeatitis, PLEASE call this emergency hotline: 1-800-OFF-BEAT. You and/or your "friend" can talk anonymously to any one of our counselors. (However, our hours are limited as none of the staff actually have Offbeatitis and are usually out enjoying a normal social life.)

PLEASE – take a moment to look at the photos off all these special people with Offbeatitis. Most of the children could have been saved if caught early on; however, their idiot parents made their children listen to music no one else in the neighborhood was listening to instead of buying HIP-HOP like every other good urban parent. If the parents of ridiculously rare children would have let their young ones sleep with the radio in their beds to help set their impressionable brainwaves to the 2-4 rhythm, instead of being corrupted by heavy metal where there's virtually no bass drum or synchronization, at all, we might have been able to improve their high school social life by thirty seven percent. However, many parents hated the thought that they got pregnant so young and figured if they have to be seen in undergrad with their sons and daughters they would prevent any chance of them being competition for Homecoming King or Queen.

We have installed hidden cameras and witnessed many of these sick parents sneaking into their children's bedrooms to ensure their children's ill-social-fate. We watched while these evil spirited adults (carrier of the Offbeatitis gene) abruptly yanked the radio cord out of the Offbeatitis victim's wall socket in the middle of the night; had they been caught these children might have had a decent survival rate.

Once the cord was cut, prematurely, most of the adolescent's brains were in mid download and we suspect stopped on the "off" beat. So in essence, the children aren't "off" beat, they just aren't adequately equipped to finish what they started.

-MESSAGE!-

Studies show that if victims of Offbeatitis could find the *exact* song that was playing when their nighttime radio cords were cut, and the *exact* part of the song, at the *exact* second the song was ripped from their heads, they **might** have a chance to regain their rhythm!

By sending in just $19.99 a month, less than $1 a day, *you* could help prevent Offbeatitis from spreading to the next generation. Extensive research show children born with or who have been affected by Offbeatitis have a 65% chance of not surviving middle school.

With your monthly donation, we will be able to send the child or adult you choose to adopt an iPod filled with thousands of songs with heavy percussion. If you adopt an Offbeatitis patient today, as a bonus we'll download several music videos with heavy choreography including videos by Ciara, Janet Jackson, Britney Spears, Beyonce and Usher (Chris Brown was dropped from this endorsement).

If you're one of the first 100 sponsors to call in, we'll include a personal trainer to come to your patient's house after they've completed their 6-week online course (available for $29.00 the first month and $50.00 each additional month) to assess their progress and share helpful tips on overcoming Offbeatitis.

Call NOW and we'll, even, throw in free web support and access to our blog to post success stories! (We guarantee no such thing.)

Call in RIGHT now! Your Offbeatitis recipients are waiting on you to lift them off the ground when they fall flat on their faces and break their noses; when they hit their heads; trip over their feet while looking at someone else on the dance floor.

Please - Help remove the chaotic, embarrassing behavior out of the lives of Offbeatitis victims and one day they will finally find their place back to the natural rhythm of life!

roach motel on central drive

I've decided
to go back to school
and, uh ...
my roommate and I
have roaches

At first, it was just one;
with balls.
I was told not to "worry" about it,
it's only one roach,
it comes with the territory.

What territory?
Poverty?!
Like they have a secret
roach society
that peeps out low income areas
and attacks
like they know we're going to leave
food out for them:
chicken not put away
spaghetti still left in the pot
from last night
remains on plates from a late night
snack.

I am so glad the Orkin commercial had a white lady
with roaches
in section of what bugs
they can exterminate
We all know it was fake.
A cover up;
The token Negro in the marketing department was like
"Hey...uh, Tom, Dave,
I don't think we should put a black person in the roach
commercial.
Let's save them for, uh...termites.

We can do something cool and unexpected;
like the little boy playing drums or something diverse!
But, yeah, uh, having black people in the roach section
would be a little cliché, don't you think? Tom? Dave?"
Then we saw his cousins;
Yes, roaches have cousins.
One over the door in the bathroom
A Peeping Tom roach
A look-out roach,
running back to tell the crew
when we were home and shit.

You know when you have roaches, bad,
when:
they start making you tip-toe
around *your* house!
Turning on the lights
from around the corner,
peering into each room
to see how many buggers
are out just partying.

You know you have roaches, bad,
when:
you jump back
every time you open your cabinet doors
just in case a roach pops out
like "Oh, damn… I didn't hear you coming,
my bad!"

Then you see one
on a glass
you try not to make eye contact,
and you're trying not to imagine
all of the roaches climbing
in and out of all the glasses, in your cabinet;
you try not to imagine them
walking around
on all the silverware in the drawers

You can't help it, though;
it's like you're frozen stuck
staring at the roach
trying not to imagine all the gross stuff
he and the cousins were doing.

One day, I decided to get some ammo:
Raid!
First: Why is the roach spray in the grocery section?
Right next to the BBQ Potato Chips!
I thought roach spray would be in: Lawn and Garden.
No – they didn't even try to cover up
the fact that roaches are kitchen infiltrators
Second: There are eighty different kinds of roach killing
products!
There's the tape. Right.
Like your house guests
wouldn't notice white tape stuck
to your floors and walls with dead roaches
hanging on them; and you're talkin' 'bout,
"No… they aren't real.
That's the new home décor
Feng shui motif originated in Thailand.
It's a new design; just came out this year.
I saw it on HGTV last night!"

Then there's my favorite;
the roach smoke bomb!
These are the directions:
cover up everything in your house,
take all the food
out of your cabinet,
close all the windows,
put the bombs in the middle of each room
you want to fumigate,
pull the pin on the bomb
and you have 30 seconds to get out of your house.
Leave the bombs in there for an entire day,
then, one hour before reentering,
open all the windows.

Ok: A - how you are going to open
all the windows *before* you enter?
And B - Like your same neighbors won't notice
the entire family
diving for the car to escape the bombs
going off in your house;
smoke seeping out of the windows
like an Iraqi war zone.

"It's us against the roaches!"

And didn't "They" say that roaches
would be the only thing to survive
World War III?
So why in *thee* hell would three Raid bombs in your house kill
them?
Unless there's something in those Raid Bombs
ATF isn't telling us;
could be another conspiracy
to kill off all people
who live in low income areas.

Inside the secret military meeting:
"Ok, here's what we're going to do – we're going to plant
roaches in all the low income areas
where there's poverty, people of color –
Oh, wait! That'd be the same place!
Ok, and people on welfare
with no medical coverage –
Oh, wait! All that's in one area!
We can set the roaches free
on the Lower East Side!
The roaches will infiltrate their kitchens, spread
throughout their homes. We'll blackmail
Raid into creating a Roach Bomb and market it
to grocery stores in impoverished areas. Then we'll secretly
replace the smoke with CB4! Making them lazy and killing them
slowly.

Then one day I decide to grab:
Instant Roach Aerosol Killer.
Kills on contact!
They don't have a chance to escape.

I was cleaning the kitchen,
which is how this whole thing started;
a roach emerged from the dirty dishes,
I grabbed the can.
No time to run!
Shake
spray
and he's dead!

Roaches are so dramatic
that's why they end up in so many movies
they have the best dying scenes
they spin around three times
and die on their backs with their feet in the air
still kicking
Still kicking?!
This is why I got the can!
I beat the crap out of the roach with the edge of the can!
I didn't even want to give them a chance
to resuscitate their cousins!
Yes, roach resuscitation!
I can hear them screaming, now: "Don't die, Jimmy! Don't die!"

I scrub and move all the seasonings
out of the cabinet to clean up the spills,
You know that every time you put a seasoning
back in the cabinet,_it spills out a little;
then you have a little sand pile of Old Bay and Lawry's
Imagine all the roaches building Cayenne Pepper sand castles
swimming in the hot sauce,

The ones from the south like spicy food
and originated in New Orleans. Yes, all southern roaches
originated New Orleans.
The ones with the wings? Florida.

The Mexican roaches prefer the Adobe section
of your cabinets. Those little brown specs
in the rice, you think is the natural
discoloration of the grain —
Oh, no! It's not called dirty rice for nothing!

Northern roaches, in New York and
Chicago — industrial
pet size roaches
that cling
to the side of your wall,
helping you do homework,
looking over your shoulder
whispering:
"Hey,
Hey!
Psssssst! That math problem is wrong.
You might want to review that
before turning it in, tomorrow. Oh, and your boyfriend
had that ho from English class over here, earlier
before you got off work. I wouldn't
be going around giving him no head, if I were you.
My cousin, that sits on top of the door
in the bathroom
said she stank and had some sort of itch."

MESSAGE!

Clean up your life and you won't
have to worry about unwanted
guests.

the real period poem
inspired by real life events. really.

When I get to heaven
I am kicking Eve's ass!

Bitch! God said
Don't - mothafreakin'- touch the - mothafreakin apple!!
And what did yo' bitch-ass do?!
Touch the - mothafreakin - apple!

Burst into flames, Eve!

You know that commercial with the chick on the bus with her
dress stuck in her underwear?!
1: Like she didn't feel the breeze under that tiny ass skirt and
2: Ain't nobody wearing all white on day two of our cycles!

Misconception about periods,
it's not day one that is the monster;
day one is the warning
The get out all your fat and dark clothes
for the next five to seven days
I am here to ruin:
your life
relationship
and risk your children being sent off
to Social Services
Your friends & family
will think you're trying out for a part in the Exorcist!

Not that your, independent,
nose stuck up in the air, ass was fucking
anyway, but this week
it's a wrap.
You better wear latex gloves
If you even *think* about masturbating!
Ever heard of the red sea?

That's me!
Part the waves
'cause I'm coming in strong!

Get it in, now, on day one
'cause two through seven
(oh yes, seven! I saw you eat that entire can
of Grands Biscuits last week; you knew
I was coming
and bread is *not* a friend to the period cycle;
the more carbs, the worse the cycle;
get it together, you could use a gallon of water
anyway; look at that gut!)

Day one is the precursor for the wrath to come;
day two is the beast!

The, you better be in the best health of your life
or taking some gangsta-ass vitamins (week);
otherwise you'll have to stand.

You'll have to stand
during your entire period!

Uh, uh, you can't sit down and risk
having the ever-so-embarrassing
spot
on the back of your clothes
that all your haters
won't tell you about

Oh, no.

They'll let you walk around
with that fucking spot
on the back of your clothes, all day!

They'll keep calling you over
to ask you, annoying ass, questions

so you have to get up from your cube
and walk 48 miles
in slow motion
across the office floor
to answer them:

"Hey do you know if the boss is coming back from lunch?
How much more vacation time do you have?
Did you hear about the lay-offs?"

Sure, you can take meds,
then you'll be either hyper and bloody, spewing blood
from your vagina all over the insides
of your legs, making your crotch
all mushy
while you bounce around, all day, as if
you're on 14 shots of espresso
Or:
You can take the meds that make you sluggish
that leave you lying in blood
for five days.
You don't move;
you're depressed
which makes you go to the bathroom less,
you change your napkins less

Then you get: Toxic Shock Syndrome!

Great.
The drugs make you a zombie and eventually kill you
via: Toxic Shock Syndrome!
There you have it.
Your period can kill you!

And/or give you a yeast infection.
You're walking around smelling
like a swamp of dead rats
and seaweed bread.

Women should get temporary handicap stickers
for three out of the four weeks in a month!

We're not on our periods for just five days!
No-way mothafuckers!
We're on our periods for three whole weeks!

The week *before* our period:
this is the week we eat everything
in the house
and scream at everyone
for – breathing!

Then you cry.
About everything.
And you start to pair things
that don't even go together
like: you're crying because Oprah
is on and you can't find your car keys
And even though Oprah's show
has nothing to do with relationships, today
you've now decided to end
your perfectly good relationship
because your car keys symbolize
your inability to mobilize
on your own!
You now feel dependent
on your car
and gas;
and since gas is so high
you think you're a loser
because your credit score is fucked up
you can't afford gas so, you're walking
down your block
crying
mascara streaking
shirt wrinkled and ruined
from whipping your eyes
'cause using tissue is killing

trees in (insert your city here)
you're afraid the little boy, across the street
dying of cancer
won't be able to breathe
if you continue using tissue!

Keys in hand
tethered shirt
melted make-up
and barefoot
(because you're now a vegan)
you head to the bus stop
(which, you've never actually taken before)
and it begins to pour
Not just regular rain;
pour.
You're laughing, hysterically
'cause someone told you
rain is God's way of blessing you
You're cupping the rain
with your hands
spinning around in circles
knocking over small children and
stepping on animals.
Folk at the bus stop
are slowly backing away
from you

This was last week.
The week of warning.
You ignore it
like every month
put on a short white skirt
and proceed to get on the bus?
Doubt it.

The week of bleeding, that's always nice.
It'd be different if we could control
where our periods were going to start
(like we can control when).

If we knew
periods were going to come
while we were at home,
that'd be a lot better
than the ever panic
of having to carry around
a separate change of clothes, like we're creepin'!
We have to explain to our partners, once a month
why the hell we have an extra gym bag full of clothes
and no membership.
It's not like we can really wear any of our clothes.
Ever.
Our closet ranges from:
your size to 146
thousand;
depending on the week.
The period uniform? Baggy shirt and jeans from pregnancy.
Black only.
Before people catch on to your monthly wardrobe shift, they'll
think you're a black panther
trying to hold on
to the dream and may randomly approach you
with their fists in the air.
If you live in (insert very white suburb of your city, here), they'll
think you're a Goth chick.

During this week of blood whenever speaking
with someone,
use an old super model's trick:
Stand with your writing hand leg
behind you
to peel off 10 pounds
by pure illusion!

Try **not** to have short conversations. People will wonder
why you're standing
with one leg back,
sucking in your stomach,
wildly batting your eyes,
holding a gym bag.

It took me 14-hours, last time, before they let me go
on my own recognizance.
I tried to tell them, black women,
although often suspected, are not known
for serial murders.
Random murders; yes!
Serial; no.
We don't have to time
to pick a fucking pattern,
we have cramps!

The week after our periods,
we're trying to deflate and lose
the two weeks of weight we gained,
and clear up our skin from all the junk food and toxins.
There is, really, only have one week of normalcy.
Hey son...uh, what are you doing???
Son: Home....work....
Period victim: Don't fucking breathe
so fucking loud.
Don't fucking talk.
Don't move.
As a matter of fact, don't fucking move
for the next three years!
Go to your room!
You're grounded for-EVER!

Son on phone with social services: My mom's on her period
ag... Hello? Hello?
Period victim's at son's door with cut phone cord
in one hand and cell phone battery in the other.
I'll get with you after I finish this: pickle, sardine,
peanut butter, chicken leg on rye, potato chip with mustard
ice-cream, rum and coke sandwich young man!

Periods should give us a temporary insanity pass.

Periods are responsible for: 82% of 12% of the 49,000
43 and a half billion people
that have alcoholism.

And that make shit up.

What the fuck do we have cramps for?
Right. Eve.
Burst into flames, bitch!
KILL YOURSELF!

Hold on while I eat four more whole fried chickens.

You're in the shower
there are blood clots falling on the floor
and all of a sudden it's not romantic
to have sex in the shower, any more!?!

You're the ones that want to fuck
on our period
with your greedy-ass!
You, my friend, have low self-esteem;
you figure we'd automatically be wet
and you can brag to your friends how good it was.

Was it?
Really?
Who knew?
Not me!
You think we can feel you
with a pint of blood gushing between our legs?
You think you've done something here?
Clearly not.

Tampons?
An evil man
thought of tampons.
He just wanted to imagine us
playing with our vaginas.
Dear, pervert; You think inventing expanding tampons
is preparation for when we're horny as hell
the day after our periods?
You made those things to expand in our vaginal walls

for your penis? Really?
I think an 18 pound baby is bigger
than your fucking dick
and if we can take that for 24 hours straight
I don't think you need to invent any-fucking-over sized,
yeast infection carrying, Q-tip
to stretch us into shape!

You wonder why we hate men and kids!
Oh – Don't get it twisted – we hate them both!

Choices?!
Oh, we got choices.
Either walk around with a mini dick in our vagina
for five days,
a cup that'll spill over onto our clothes,
a mini-diaper,
or sentenced to 80 years of children?!?
Great fucking choices, Eve!
Bloody clothes, mood swings for three weeks,
a yo-yoing weight and scale
or kids?!
Great.
Thanks a fucking lot, Eve!
I hope you choke on an apple seed, bitch!

Those commercials are a joke!
Happy women,
all wearing white
chatting about the latest whatever the fuck…
What are they doing while chatting?
You got it, standing up
at a party,
 at a club,
or at a bar;
even the chick on the bus
with her damn skirt in her ass,
(like she couldn't feel that shit),
was probably distracted with the mini dick

in her twat, bouncing around
on a shitty city bus.
The government should allow women
free plumbing for all the pipes we clog up
with our napkins.

Oh, sure,
we can wrap them up in toilet paper
like our mommies taught us.
Just so I'm clear - I'm supposed to leave dried blood
seeping through thin cheap tissue in my trash can
and pack a gun
for all the buzzards hovering outside
my bathroom windows and rats
sniffing their way through the pipes,
into our apartments and homes
searching out that smell of freshly-dried-blood?
Nice.

Then, of course, you have the entire neighborhood
of cats in your backyard
and on top of your roof
and under your car, trying to trap the mice and rats
your dried blood
has lured them to.

Dogs barking at the cats, following me
to the bus stop,
sniffing my crotch.
I'm trying to convince the other passengers
it's a seeing eye dog
that needs my scent.
We end up being the fucking Dr. Doolittle –slash– Pied Piper
of the fucking wild kingdom.

Now, PETA is at my door
talkin' 'bout how I killed fluffy
who was sleeping under my car
to keep warm, at night.

Shit. I got bad luck
for nine years,
cats keeping me awake a night,
rats scratching at my pipes and air ducts, and buzzards
lurching in the trees.
On a bright sunny 72 degree Georgia afternoon
I have to leave my house
with full body armor and an umbrella to
avoid being killed by the wild
'cause of my period.

I show up at my shrink
and she says I'm making up the buzzards
in the trees and gives me Seroquel XR
for schizophrenia.

As I'm leaving the pharmacy,
they told me to make sure I:
stand on my head,
with one arm out
avoid direct sunlight
and if at all possible air *and* water
'cause Seroquel XR can cause cancer
of the arm
and I could die in my sleep
if taken incorrectly.
If I feel any nausea, urges to gamble, see pink elephants, have
trouble communicating, sudden pregnancy or death;
I should contact my physician immediately.

And if I can't afford these medications,
AstraZeneka may be able to help.

haiku: for m.i.a.

Arizona; fly.
racism, classism, break.
Genocide. Freedom.

ESPN: - extra special poets network

Imagine it!
A stadium of 10 thousand screaming fans
A stage in each end zone
A 5-mic full sound system set–up,
complete with flashing lights,
smoke and theme music
upon entry of each opposing team!

Sponsorship banners hang from the stands:
Yahoo groups – the official sponsor for poetry mass
communication!
Southwest Airlines – the only airline poets can really afford!
Composition Notepads – if you've never written in a
composition, you've never written!
Greyhound – the way poets who are "keeping it real" travel!
Memorex, TDK and Maxell – blank CDs for poets who refuse to
get their albums printed professionally and continue to burn on
their laptops!

Commentating tonight's bouts are ESPN favorites:
Bob – I don't know shit about poetry and
Tom – I needed this gig to keep my job!
Two of the most disconnected people from poetry ever!

We need more people in the seats at a poetry venue, right?
Television is the only thing that validates anyone's existence
what better way to get poetry out to people who couldn't really
care less?
Monopolize the airwaves!

B: Good to see you here tonight, Tom.

T: Yes, Bob, this is the first Poetry Slam ever aired on ESPN,
and the station decided to risk its entire ratings for the evening
to appease these geeks!
B: The teams are backstage warming up. I think I heard them
chanting Kumbaya. Was that a peace pipe?

T: It was pretty strong, Bob; it was a piece of something. In all seriousness, these teams have competed all year long for... bragging rights? Did I read that correctly? We have an error on the monitor; it reads, 'Bragging rights'. Who wrote this?

B: No million-dollar endorsements?

T: Somebody needs to get a hold of their managers. Tonight's competition brings us to the final four teams in the nation!: Team - Always does political poems, up first. Followed by Team - We really wanted to be comedians, up second. In the third slot is Team - We die at the end of all our poems. And, in the favored fourth position, is Team - We think we're the poetic elite with such accreditations as Cave Canem and Bar 13.

B: Team Political is sending up a heavy hitter; she's set to do an old favorite. They're so well spoken! It sounds like Rap, Tom!

T: Wait! She's doing a new poem! Does she have clearance for that? Where's her Poetry Approval Form in triplicate? Has that poem been cleared by the FCC? The FAA? The ACLU? The CIA? The FBI? The Intel Headquarters? Channel 5? Ground Zero?

B: Oh, my goodness, Tom! She's cursing! Cut to commercial! Cut to commercial!

Commercial Break: After Love Jones, the spike in poetry venues across the country was prolific. News reports called it, "The Newest in the Black Power Movement." "The Civil Rights activists are back!" "Beatnik poetry returns!" "The Underground comes up for air!"

10 years later,
you'd be hard pressed to find ten consistent venues
that last ten weeks for less than $10.

T: And we're back. The teams have been warned about their language. From here on out, if they violate any of the 286 restrictions set forth by their contractual agreement to be aired on ESPN they and/or their teams, depending on the level of severity, will be immediately disqualified!

B: Team Political was given a penalty for free speech and has been warned.

T: That's right, Bob. No free speech here; sponsors pay for that! (Both chuckle.)

B: Next up, Comic rejects!

T: This should be good; they have the advantage of humor. That's why this is the sports channel; no one wants to remember they're a loser. It gives them a chance to live vicariously through the athletes, in this case, the poets. He has three minutes on the clock, and he's off. Wonderful posture...

B: Yes, his stage presence is incredible! Look how he's drawing the crowd in... Wait! Wait! Did you hear that?

T: What'd he say about my mama? Cut to commercial! Cut to commercial!

Commercial Break: Promoters book comedians to host poetry shows for draw. Promote an after party to entice a crowd unprepared for what they're getting into.
What was once promoted for diversity and culture
is now a fight for power, status quo and popularity.
The best way to get people to forget their problems is to
make them laugh, make them forget their issues... even if for just three minutes.

T: We're back again. The sponsors are dropping out in rapid numbers; the ratings are dropping. I'm not sure if we're going to make it through the first round, Bob. There are no scores on the board and two teams have penalties against them. Let's see what the Suicide poets do.

B: They shouldn't have any problems getting through their pieces, especially if they die before they make any violations. (Both force out a stiff ha-ha-ha-ha.)

T: Boy, I hope my family is not watching this fiasco. What in the world were they thinking, talking all that truth! I can't have my children exposed to that type of language!

T: The poet takes the stage... Oh, my goodness, is there a drug screening?

B: He looks like death! Why is he wearing all black? Didn't that go out in the 60's? Here's his poem...

B: What is he saying? He's talking so low... What is that? A knife? Is that ketchup? Cut to commercial! Cut to commercial!

Commercial Break: Thousands of people who've discovered the art of poetry have added theatre and drama into their works. Many poets find this form of expression quite the alternative for the real thing. Unofficially, poetry has saved the lives of thousands of people due to being inspired by or creating art.

B: Well, Tom, the Suicide poets have also taken a penalty for using props. Props are not allowed in a poetry slam — only what you can use with your own body and anything available on the stage.
T: And he received a low score mostly because that was the first and only poem completed tonight. The crowd is getting restless... what's left of it. People are starting to file out. I don't think this is what the audience had in mind. I think they expected blood and guts from a poetry 'slam.'

B: You're right, 'slam' is misleading; there's no slamming going on, only harmless poetry. It looks like whoever gets the highest score between the Suicide poets and this last round by the Pseudo-Elite poets will win tonight's championship tournament.

T: It's a shame those other teams sacrificed their chance at winning for the sake of true expression.

B: Yeah, Tom, in 'real' sports, athletes consistently sacrifice their integrity for fame. These poets better get with the program, if they ever really want to be recognized.

T: Here's the final poet of the evening… Wow! She's reading from paper! Is that allowed in a competition?

B: Well, if there's no official rule, there should definitely be some point deduction! Reading off paper can't be professional…

Interjection: Although most commentators are familiar with most athletes and their stats, commentators habitually read from paper, monitors and cue cards when giving a news report to keep all the stats straight, especially when giving stats on a rookie, MVP or high school athlete in their uh… professions.

T: I can barely understand what she's saying… What is she talking about? Do you get double points for big words?

B: She needs to be on ESPN Scrabble Channel. How do the judges score what they don't understand? You need a dictionary to decipher what she's saying… Wow! We made it through with no penalties!

T: The judges didn't seem to get it, either. Ooh,… low 5's and 6's for the Pseudo-Elite poetry team. Wait! What is she doing!? She's back on the stage, throwing her notebook at the judge's pit!

B: Security to Stage 2! Security to Stage 2! The Pseudo-Elite will be disqualified for violating code 26.8.t.squared-A-L-46 of their contract – "No unnecessary roughness."

(Side comment) Commercial Break?
Nope! No commercial break… They deserved that one!

T: That's all from the Office Max Super Dome, Office Max, a poet's super supply store! Looks like Team We die at the end of all our poems wins the match tonight!

B: Well, it goes to show you, even death is better
than being disqualified for
sacrificing self-expression!

james

James was a good man
James had a
job
with that total
Mike Peace house nigga' type package
Now -
James was a good man
James woke
at the same time
every day.
He wore the same black-blue-gray
industrialized
smoke inhibited suit

James was a good man.

He polished
the same six pair of black shoes
that blazed the
same path to work.
Holding his employer's paraphernalialized
coffee mug
with only four fingers
at a time to keep them
from burning,
slightly
His breath blew gentle icicles
over the lid.

The same people passed James
on his path
Now –
James was a good man.
He didn't catch
the summer twitch or
the cold lonely itch

Now, James was a good man;
in 23 years he never was a late
to work.
His lunches were exactly 29
imprisoned minutes
his feet didn't return on his
worn dirt path home
until the faint click of the red
digital clock flipped its
plastic numbers to 5 p.m.
Now, James was a good man.
On his way home
something caught his eye
In the distance he could hear
faint
music
The city had grown up
around him
the music was pulsating
through the early evening air
beckoning his presence
The two mile walk
he started in 1964
when 'Peace' was the word
and your brotha' was your brotha
and your sista' was a
brown-honey-suckle-cinnamon-twist
so sweet
you checked every man
that came to bring her ice cream
and sit on the front step of your mama's
blue bottom house;
the one that if your sista' rocked too hard
in the porch swing,
she might shake a shingle loose

Now –
James was a good man

Tonight he looked up
from the rhythmic patter splat
heel toe
heel toe
heel toe
pattern that beat the cracked concrete
in his shiny black shoes
1987 brought a new life
to the city that grew up
around him
Now, James was a good man
Malcolm was dead
Martin had long since become a national holiday
for the wrong reason
and Mandela
was still in jail
this night was a new revolution
James stopped counting his steps
3,044
45
46
looked right past the tint
into the window
arms flying in the air
the Wop
Cabbage Patch
Roger Rabbit
Reebok
Running Man
and the Prep
were simulated under
intoxicated influence

James was a good man.

He noticed her
gold bronze arms
winding and
bouncing

in the reflection
of the disco ball
waving,
not sporadically,
slowly
twisting
and twirling;
capturing
the trails of smoke clouds
and pulling them
to make mini cyclones
around her body.

She found James' eye
It was like she already knew
he was there before he decided
to stop and stare
into that
new
glass
window
The people,
captured, in the frame
were still
dancing;
she seemed to
float
she glided
right through the crowd
that bounced
gyrated and popped
all around her

Somehow she appeared
directly in front of James
on the sidewalk
There weren't any words
she slid her long brown fingers
through his large hands

looked him straight in the eye
and winked
softly
He couldn't help but stare;
James was a good man.

Because, James was a good man
his eyes studied
the red three-layer dress
ruffles at the ends
It hugged her body
like a newborn's grip
around his mother's index finger
Her hair was natural;
a soft afro
freshly shaped
into a halo.
When the wind picked up, a little
James could smell the African-peach
shampoo
When she walked
her stride was so
long
It seemed as if she left
the last leg, behind
for three whole seconds
before her hips shifted
and rotated
the other around to the front

Because, James was a good man;
they were in his room
Because, James was a good man;
they were standing
in the middle
of his floor
his clothes fell off
somewhere
up the last five steps

she stood under his chin
barefoot in her dress
he looking down at her
she up at him
both sets of limbs
hanging
by their sides; as if locked
in an invisible case
his arm bent, slowly
when he reached down
and slid off one spaghetti strap
Leaning forward,
his brown lips
pressed against her red gloss

He pulled away
effortlessly.

James
took both hands
slid them down
the sides of her dress
with only his index fingers
He lifted the ends of her
red ruffles, around the mocha curves
of her bottom
slipped his fingers on the
insides of her panties
slid his hands on the insides
of her thighs
and pressed down
The silky satin slid
to the floor
in
slow
motion.

The dress followed.

Both looked down
at the dark red
weaving between their feet,
stepped
over the clothes
and fell into bed.
She on her back; he crawled
on top of her
Parted her legs with one knee
took
both of her wrists
with one hand;
pulled them
above her head
his other, he placed
on her shoulder

Entering her,
she took
a quick
breath
the sound a gas stove makes
when you put a match to it
James realized this was the first time
he heard her voice.
The hand around her wrists
tightened
The other
slid from her shoulder, down the center
of her breasts
He flattened his palm
against the waves of her stomach
around to the small of her back
forcing an arch
gave permission
to go further inside
His stroke:
faster
his grip on her wrists:

stronger
tighter
un-releasing
his hand traveled
from her back
up around the dents of her throat
and pressed down
he forced his tongue
in her mouth
searching hers
her head twisted violently
back and forth

twisted violently back and forth
twisted violently back and forth
twisted violently back and forth
twisted violently back and forth

declining
his touch

her legs
unraveled from the pretzel
position around his back
beating her heels
down
on the back of his calves and thighs
His advance
inside her
didn't rest;
he forced his position
painfully
around the residence
of her wisdom
the grip on her throat
became constricted
she let out short gags
and stared back
in those same eyes

that were so inviting
only minutes ago
James buried his head
in her shoulder and pressed
on

laborious thrusting
promised to break her
Her last few gasps
echoed in the room
his head snatched fiercely back
creating a reverse slope
in his spine
her legs twitched
next to James
three
more
times
before her carcass
when limp
beneath him

James released
with a bellowing
that found its way
over city blocks
to the club
People on the dance floor froze
mid-Wop
they thought they heard
something
her body, lifeless
and James screamed on.

released for:
everyday he was on time to work
everyday he never left early
everyday he made his family wait
every child support check he ever signed

every weekend his children
went back to their mother and new
extremely rich
step-father
on time;
for taking the same route to work for 23 years
for never looking up
for shutting the window
on his lunch break, as a million
men marched
outside his office that weekend
for getting the same raise percentage
for wearing the same shoes
the same suit
for having 84 sick days on the books
for turning down his
secretary's innocent offer
to dinner
eight times
for saying "Yes sir,"
when he wasn't right,
to his boss 184,368 times
this year
for always having exact change
for every bill being paid on time
for changing the ink cartridge
in the copier
every time someone walked away
with the light blinking:
TONER IS LOW!
TONER IS LOW!
TONER IS LOW!

For paying his taxes
voting at every local election
for reading the labels
on the back of every product
he ever bought
for getting his hair cut

every Friday at 6:30 by ole' Fred
for every murder
in his neighborhood
he read about
every morning
at the same coffee table
in the same chair
folded the paper
back to it's original form
then walked to work.
James brought his head back down
began breathing sporadically
looked at the woman
lifeless
in his bed

Naked
standing
facing his mirror
he used two fingers
opened the top drawer
and brought the gun to his head

In two seconds
what the carpet didn't catch
slid down the mirror
writing it's last love letter
reflecting
back at the room
infinite times

James' body conceded,
the sound of his bones
crushing against the foundation
like your upstairs neighbor
throwing 100 pair of shoes
on the floor above you
the gun fell
somewhere
Two weeks later, the police
pushed open his door

with the butt of their guns
K-9 lead to investigate
a smell
reported by the neighbors.

Hidden in plain sight
James' body
on the floor;
the mirror
finger painted in blood;
the police found nothing
in his house
touched;
only a pair of red panties
placed on a neatly made bed

Now,

James was a good man.

haiku: for john s. blake

Malcolm and Jesus
needles trump nails
fight dirty; both found by the rocks.

Shots were fired

not exactly the butterfly effect

Love is like the flutter of cockroach wings;
you can feel it before you see it.
By then, it's too late; it's all over you.
And no matter what
you can't shake it.
You're impaled
thinking about it days later.

by default

It's not that I don't **love** you
I love you – I mean
I don't want you to get hit by a bus
or anything
that would definitely ruin my day

I just don't have that flutter of
let me freshen up
fix my hair
fluff the pillows and throw a whole banana nut loaf
in the oven
to pretend
I have exemplary culinary skills
light smelly candles
sprinkle books
around the house and let the sleeves of porno tapes
peek out from the shelves
you know, so you think
I'm well rounded

sprawl out
on the couch in my boy shorts
and tank top that hold my breasts
just right
take 30 extra seconds
to get to the door
open it up, all casual
lean on the molding
hold it open with one arm
imply with my eyes
you're, totally, interrupting
my oh-so-rare me-time
all while giving you
that twisted mouth smile
revealing I would have started without you
had you taken too long

to pretend
you "happen to be in the neighborhood"

Yeah, I just don't get that feeling about you
Figures –
angels require too much
paperwork
to mend a heart
that's lost its elasticity
I'd settle
for a Fix-A-Flat
and just count the beats
while we watch this whole thing
deflate

You don't want me (honey) chyle
I treat my lovers like binges
in my eating disorder
The added calories don't count
if there's no witness
to the consumption

I waited for the ponies and princes
the first touch
glance, look, stare
and we marry
in some 24HR attorney's office
with more paperwork
per square foot than walk space
He forgets our name
in the ceremony
the horse
in front of the carriage, outside
has Alzheimer's
and arthritis
called it a night
leaving us
to a smelly dollar cab
with my second hand wedding dress

caught in the door
dragging through the streets
tethered and Holy
by the time we reach the hotel
we cleared our savings for
Two nights on the 12th floor
including breakfast

I waited for the one knee
in the Dr.'s office
when we thought we were pregnant
and it turned out to be final exam stress

I waited for (the) we reached
for the same coffee mug
across the table
at the truck stop diner
neither of us looking up
from our morning papers
Mine - a tabloid
with aliens on the front.
Yours - the local Journal
with aliens on the front

I waited for the blind-fold
drive me around aimlessly
for hours
hop a chartered plane
land
on an island
and pop the question
in our double-VIP-extended-lounge-all inclusive-suite
with Pierre at our every beck and call
Even if I pretended
to be coy
your psychic
we are the world
soul mates
prick a finger

blood in a locket
BFF
channeling
should have told you different

Don't tell me
I'm fantasizing
Don't tell me
I'm waiting
for something that'll never happen
That's the expectations
you laid out in your rap songs
right?
That's what you said
us, "down bitches" would get
right?

Oh come on! Don't
twist your face up now
I would have never brought up
the damn jet
had you not said
you had one "on deck"
I would have been good with the transit but, you…
You, homey, hyped the shit up
about extravagant shopping sprees
and spontaneous get a ways

I just wanted stability
a place I could come home to
and not have to lie
about my return date
arriving a day early
to catch you in the act
I don't want to have to oil the floorboards
and tip-toe
through the backdoor of *our* home
because of something Keisha emailed me about

I just want to rest in your arms
crash on your chest
I'm breaking up with you by default
Habit, really
Why ruin a good thing
Lets face it
no one's showing up
to fill my side of the pews
Who should I invite
People who already know
I loathe you

I waited for the
tall, short, fat, thin, fit, asthmatic, sumo wrestler, kite flying
champion stock holder, sand castle builder, polygamist,
monogamist, bare-foot, self searching inner-spirituality, finding
solace in a peanut butter and jelly sandwich, backpacks
through Europe, reading, *Malachi York for Dummies*, incense
falling out of his backpack, while checking his PDA
But, I met you
at a party
while I was on a date

Let's just call a spade
a knife to my throat
a paper cut to my jugular
You know the old saying
If the shoe fits
buy a pair two sizes smaller
I'm not the marrying kind, anyway
well, at least, no one asked me

My life's not that simple
I mean, you're all stable
Me
Over 28 part-time jobs
14 homes
in twice as many years

I like moving around
it makes me feel like a spy

Used goods
I think they call it

You're all responsible
Me
A credit score
lower than a decent performance stipend
You're all calm
Me
I got: OCD, ADHD, Adult ADD
restless leg syndrome
acid reflux disease
I have a Tempurpedic -slash- sleep number bed
and have given night watch jobs
to all the unemployed Serta sheep

You're all
yeah, yeah
all the things I prayed for
yada-yada
I didn't mean literally
dammit
You need some edge
Some spontaneity
Some phony scene
about pills
that'll help boost
our sex drive
You pretending
to wash the cars
I flip my sandals
over my freshly manicured toes and
bat my eye lashes
over top of a book
I stopped reading chapters ago

I want to look forward to
drumming myself up
for the remote possibility
of being excited
about you over my tongue
punishing my wind pipe
But, your taste is like communion
dull and pointless
Unless, of course, you believe
swallowing the flesh
is equivalent to love

We shouldn't be with someone because no one else wants us

We become who we fear
The thing we tend to forget is
we're our own experts
and can call it quits
whenever we feel like it
without, you know, regret
zero body count

God knocking down the towers, in the Bible
might have been a mistake
we can't communicate, now

I got this thing
where I break up with people
before we even get started
like an automatic defense mechanism
It usually goes something like this
Sheba you're cool
charismatic
a genius
yada, yada
Me: Oh, yeah
I hate your socks
Beat it

Then I walk away, dramatic
like something on Lifetime
It's never, really, that clean
of a break, though
On TV, the other person
just stands there
In real life, there's usually some profanity
being hurled at my spinal cord
it just bounces off my dolphin skin
I borrowed from Flipper
It was a fair trade
I taught Flipper how to breathe deep
and stay under longer

Such is life
I was told God crosses his fingers
while playing the Lotto

When I'm angry
when my patience runs
a few seconds behind my intentions
it's only my way of saying
How dare you not be perfect
Right and exact Gabriel
Don't you know God is taking notes
in the margin
What were you thinking
showing up here
Feathers out of place
halo needs some Tarnex
Your fingertips
better not be twitching
as you kneel before Him
awaiting your next command
You've been showing up, to work
slathered
with sin on your breath
ink from the club stamp
all over your wings

I've been running behind you
screaming your name
before you jump
astonished
to find out your wings
are, only, clip-ons

My grandparents
argued daily
They haven't spoken
since the youngest left
for college
There's no need
finishing each other's sentences
when there's nothing left
to say.

the symphony

It's beautiful
the sound of crickets
outside my apartment window

Not midnight in the almost projects
government housing across the street
Us? We borrow
ghetto passes
more children than parents
here too; now a symphony of thousands
in the grass soothes them
to sleep under their pains
Plays them a lullaby
dreams of sugar plums
and big houses
with a yard
for a dog named spike

Not here, where our passes
restrict us to rent
high interest
black and lacquer
fake leather furniture
where the military
can furnish an entire house
even if they've only served for a week
we couldn't buy a lamp, on credit
after working
our civilian jobs for 10-years
at the hospital or shipyard

we're stuck
with gold fish in Muddy Waters
for pets
microwave breakfast
dinner is between music videos
you've already:

added
favorite-d
forwarded to 300 plus people
who are only your friends
behind a keyboard
Outside little green insects
rub their legs together
in harmony
while we women rub our legs
together, inside, for
survival
keeping or catching a man
to rub our shoulders
on Tuesdays and Thursdays
chase after him and cry
Monday, Wednesday and Friday
run into him
on Saturday at a party
while we were trying
to get over him
take him to church on Sunday
because, he said
he would never do it
again

While our temporary passes
gets us into house parties
it doesn't exclude us
from riding the bus
to our underpaid positions
jerking awake
four hours early
three children
take two hours
fight over one bathroom
30 seconds before the alarm
fling yourself on the hardwood
drag yourself to the bathroom
fumble for the light switch

study the unrecognizable person
in the mirror; give them your pep talk
obese city buses
arms and limbs escaping
its midsection
stop at every
irrelevant corner
railroad track and yellow light
a sigh of relief
during each break
gasping for air
hoping to relieve
a little more pressure
after each job

Our temporary memberships
don't exclude the entire family
from walking
to the grocery store
single file line
fingers red from plastic bags
cutting through the flesh
on the mile walk back
poverty replaces would-be car payments with
paying child support or
overcharged electric bills
we, who don't work
during the day
have never seen the electric company
come read the meter
and we, who travel for insurance jobs
long distance trucking
medical research and
poetry
have never noticed a difference
in the bill

The crickets still play;
play for brothers that walk their babies

double in a carriage
every morning
before standing in groups
on the corner
talking for hours
Kobe was cool
before he was caught
How dare he
mess up the Playah's Club
with a white girl, at that
play for the women
who punch pin holes in condoms
unconditional love is
nine months away
they'll fight
he'll be gone by Spring
taking her self esteem
neatly wrapped in each dime bag

they say it has to be the darkest to see the stars

over crowded living conditions
tonight, they are new lovers
he is brushing her weave
she is bagging the stash
he downs a Dos Equis and her
Sky Blue
Emotional Roller Coaster
plays on the Aiwa, new from
Wal-Mart lay-a-way

they symphony
keeps the babies sleeping
solid through the night
tummy's satisfied
oatmeal saturated milk in
Dollar Store baby bottles
they make love
without interruption

no: 11pm, 3am, 7am feedings
no spontaneous fevers
or ear infections
the music is in his subconscious
he kisses her
on the lips, for the first time
in months
then, again
on that special place
middle of her forehead
that makes women, Men In Black
forget everything
he has ever done wrong
makes us give him some
second date replay
Red Lobster
and a night drive
in love he wears a condom
in love she accepts

It's beautiful
the sound of the symphony
outside my apartment window
I sip Woodbridge while reading fiction
and pray he is safe
I will his thoughts
shift to me, just for 30 seconds
capture my smile, in freeze frame
between the memories of his
eyelids
click on: when we went swimming
during, so called, high tide
dodging jelly fish
and sea gulls plunging
from 20 feet in the air
hunting on underwater moving shadow
that proved
to be a school
of fish

looking for a cool place
to rest

Racing through the white caps of waves
crashing on our backs
he won
immediately stood
turned to encourage
my finish
rewarded me
with a forehead kiss
held me up while panting

I imagined the crickets
were calling to him, now
over the sound
of the Chesapeake Bay
on the winds
hurricanes left behind, this season
carried on music notes
played
for call girls in the 20's
rewritten in blues note
during the 60's
remixed, tonight
in house music
on cricket legs
outside my window
And maybe
maybe in those 30 seconds
he thinks of me
he'll be able to hear
the symphony.

Keep moving

untitled: haiku #23

The only problem
with a silent protest is
no one can hear you

annie

for everyone that dies before their time due to AIDS and HIV

Singing: *Darlin' rest easy the morning is coming*
Hey, hey...

similar to the lull-a-bye
my grandmother used to sing me
wrapping her wrinkled skin
around my insecurities
funny
the monster
never come from under the bed
when she was 'round

Her embrace was like the smell of cinnamon
her presence warm
her voice sweet sound waves
reverberating
and rocking me softly
'darlin rest easy the morning is coming...'

her voice bounces off my memories
adult hood would
summons the ancient chant
stored in the rolodex
of my private thoughts
recalled whenever the orange in my aura
turned purple
          slipping its way into blue

It was one of those nights in West Africa
in Accra, sunsets are the remains of mangos
placed on the equator
melted into sky paint
during the sweltering heat of the midday
spirits in Purgatory
are responsible for painting dusk

and I would pray,
as we would head north to Kumasi
the doctors in our camp
would find medicine in the leaves
pull out a miracle
like cartoon characters pulling out Acme
Why couldn't we, conveniently
find a cure in the oils
embedded in the history
of the trees
read each ring to find the answers
we've been missing?

An American;
his company sent him to work in Ghana
six months prior
one night, his wife opened the envelope
required by his company
for health benefits

      "It must be the food or the 3rd rate facilities…
      I must have touched one of them,
      or laid in their bed sheets"

uneducated about his options
he left 'round midnight
and raped five children
vowed to procure a cure
from the flower petals of a virgin

Nine and bright eyed
bigger than the soup saucers
I was forced to bring her
Annie was one of them
would bribe me
into bringing her fufu and kuskus
like most people above the status quo
she suffered from being intelligent
she said she wanted her vocabulary broadened
to speak to God in English

"He must be American, I clench my fingers until they
bleed dip my body in a stream they said was holy
I've prayed every night but he's never answered my
prayers in Twi".
"Funny," I whispered.
"I'm determined to learn Yoruba or Swahili so God will
at least recognize me."

When she wasn't sleeping
she made me a vocabulary list:
Madowu Asi
Akwaba
Etese
E-Yeah

I could barely concentrate
shaking her bed frame

 Tell me what he looks like
 I'll search the 650 million on the continent to find him!

He ripped into her hymen
butterfly razors to silk linen
killing her
with each thrust
tearing her walls
until there was bloodshed
noticed I was frustrated, she said

 "The best vengeance for our enemies
 is to let them live
 with their memories
 Their deaths will be dark
 Not dark like black
 dark like forgotten
 their souls erased
 from the history of the world;
 Besides he couldn't steal my virginity
 he may have damaged the vessel but

God saves it in a box in heaven
lined with Angel's feathers
until my wedding."

I promised to make a tiara
made of coconut hair
Why couldn't the myths be true?
Let me find a monkey's blood
for her wounds, there's no drinking bleach
to clean the disease
only AZT
and a few other drugs
reserved for the wealthy
If prolonged life is in herbs
and healthy eating
A-yo Adaabi aduante - (there is no food here)!
No nutrition
in the garbage
the Americans send us!

Urban legend lies:
Africans are not the most promiscuous
our youth program cringes
when planning a sex ed. field trip
to the free clinic
panic when students take too long
to study the survey
glance around
hide their answers
with their arms
We peel back their fingers
to reveal over 20 partners each!

I am anxious and distracted
during tonight's lesson.
How can I justify US claims
to prevent AIDS in Africa
in the same breath,
threaten to cease AID to Africa?

Our promiscuous government
fingers us in the oval office
sitcoms and reality shows
promote sexing anyone
that helps us forget
our shortcomings
the FCC that bans Sarah Jones
for female empowerment
but lets Nelly flaunt tea-bagging!?

Over 1.5 million children
(under 15)
are concerned
if they will see their parents
in the morning
their biggest worry
should be if their team
makes the play-offs for little league

Before she left me
I told her one last lie:
Masan Aba - (I'll be back)
She replied, Mabre
Eyelids stinging like needles
my logic, if I didn't move,
she wouldn't stop breathing
rocked her in the hammock
I made of fresh linen,
decorated her hair
with wild flowers,
picked out her favorite dress
and whispered Atahdea

when I close my eyes
I still see the miniature graves
where we would gather and pray

The news
came back to our camp, before we left

The American
was sentenced to death
To avoid being tortured
he confessed
he contracted AIDS at home
from his mistress
in Maryland
Careless, he put his family at risk
and blamed it on his business trip
Instead of being faithful
he gets the maximum
for his murder charges
When prisoners find out he killed
five little girls, he won't make it
past cellmate initiation
and I will be happy with that
In the Witching Hour
a noise will wake me
I know Annie has brought the children
to hear me sing:
 "darling rest easy …the morning is coming … only you know
our
           freedom…"

normal
for the survivors of 9-11

Tell me:
you were cheating on me
describe her scent
captured in the print
of your fingertips
tell me how your eyes burn
from the chemicals
of her fresh fingernail polish

Tell me:
the pores of your skin taste
the Indian Hemp in her hair
tell me how you moved under her garden
describe the shards of acrylic
embedded in the map of your back
tell me how they keloid into brail marks
branded, so I can recognize you
I'm obviously blind.

Promise me:
You were there

Tell me:
you missed James McClain and William Christmas
at San Quentin
assure me
you were not trampled
in the revolt
tell me
you were trading soap suds
with your cellmate
anything to miss the uprising

Tell me:
they set you free
for turning states evidence
and her place was the closest hideout
promise me, you were with her
suffocating in her eyes

Tell me:
time slipped by
and you forgot to leave

Tell me:
you weren't around
to see Jonathan's body
being dragged from that van
rope burning
his mid section
separating his presence,
from our history

Tell me:
you missed it;
were late getting to the civic center
where they left him

Tell me:
you were picking sugar cane
and bamboo shoots
setting Koalas free
from the local zoo

Tell me you were trapped in inspiration

Writing poems
with blueberry ink
and thorns
of a rose bush

Tell me:
you were hand sewing the bark
of ancient Willow trees
because you believe in recycling

Tell me:
you stopped to deliver
your love child
named her after your mistress and
paid her in Pomegranates
to keep it a secret

Tell me:
you robbed the local juke joint
and the quarters
made you slow

Tell me:
you are on your way to console
Myrlie, Mr. Evers's widow
drop the change in her mailbox
for their son's college fund
tell me you're not co-starring
in Medger's eulogy
I refused to believe
there were two shots
outside his home that night
Life
screaming past your ears
giving you the answers
to your mistakes
premiering on the big screen
the path you should have taken

Double Jeopardy

Tell me:
his wife didn't witness
your body orgasm
with the aftershock
of sterling silver pellets
exhausted to the concrete, face first
pebbles embedded in his cheeks
and forehead

Tell me:
You got stuck at the light
stopped
by the midnight train to Georgia
flat from the tire jaw
laid out on the road home
by the county sheriff
with K-9s trained to attack
the black in your
short sleeve shirt
tell me he gave you a ticket for
being born before '64 or
after '71
for breathing,
anything!
Just don't let
Ms. Williams, head usher on Sundays
find my phone number
you keep hidden
in you black leather gloves
invisible to the troops
at the border
searching for passports
and transfer orders
conspicuous to surgeons
searching for limbs
to your heritage

markings
of your ancestry
anything, so they know what jungle
to mail you back to

Don't let
some bars and stripes
demoted to administrative assistant
call and tell me
your number: 984
and they'll make a public
announcement
when the body count
reaches a thousand
casualties
left in the East
by a country that may grieve
but will never regret

Don't let some bitter leader
of some infantry, who secretly wishes it was him
with the purple heart,
call and tell me your body-bag
may be coming home
a little light
and, if they do find
the rest of you
will send later
with your personal effects

Tell me:
I'll be the only one to scatter
your ashes
stand
atop the freezing peeks of Denali
watch your existence

attract to snowflakes, like magnets
transform
seven times on its descent
to earth
making the patches at the mouth
of the streams
greener, where you land
soak into the soil
and trek back to Africa
underground,
like we planned

Tell me:
They drafted you
Found you
by your voter registration card
Tell me you gave them
the Rope-A-Dope, like Ali
Swam
up the Niagara to Canada
Hopped
a crop duster to Guatemala
Tell me, the physicians found Sugar[3]
in your platelets
Tell them, you are allergic to
propaganda
Tell them you missed your
swearing in ceremony
got your date mixed up with sometime next
NEVER-ARY
Will send your neighbor,
arrested four times
for domestic violence, in your place
instead

---

[3] An old skool expression for diabetes

And this morning;
this mourning, sugar
Tell me you were cheating
on me
didn't make it
to your cubical
laid so long with her
laughing at my naïveté
you missed your A-train
back to Manhattan

Tell me you left our wedding ring
on her night stand
knew I would notice
the tan line
and ran back to retrieve
my only
symbol
of sanity

Love,
tell me how you played
so long with her, in the shower
the water ran cold
through the pipes
and the steam
left indentations on your skin,
where she held you
against the tile
You two, just for a brief second
resembled African statues
originally made of ebony
mass-produced in
flea markets
passed off by peddlers as
authentic

duplicated by the thousands
collecting dust in
American homes
shipped
from illegal warehouses, in New York's
design district
worth less than Fifty Cent
on the same block, where the equal sign
stood;
towering over millions
of indigents
falsely representing
financial opportunities
for all people

Tell me you forgot your:
organizer
Palm Pilot
favorite pen
used for rejection letters, *before* the
freedom fighters
came to level the
bidding field

Tell me your skin is not
corroding next to someone's
first born
or last alive
I *don't* want to hear you
went to check on your youngest,
in daycare
don't want to hear
the ceiling is six inches
from the floor
now, you're holding
his hand

nose
scraping
against dilapidated support beams
don't want to hear
how the smoke is billowing up around you
and you can't
inhale dust particles fast enough to
commit suicide

Don't tell me you prayed not to be alive the next day
Held your nose in attempt to suffocate

Don't want to hear
you're one of hundreds
that stayed alive
for over a week;
suffocating
dying slowing
Skin turning to leather
as if you were in someone's
smoker
I swear,
I swear, if "they" ever!
turn this Holocaust
into a holiday
for:
sales and discounts
fireworks and cook-outs
a platform for any sort of
advertisement
there will be new fish to fry

I'm sure ain't no fireman
lose no life nor limb
trying to find you
You'll call

and say you let the battery
on your cell phone
run low
and I know...
I know...
you're, usually
responsible
usually,
don't let it run lower than two bars
But:
for the first time in 15 years
since I took your class ring
for the first time
since you sat with my father
on that porch swing
shaking like leaves, in the fall
applauding
you forgot
your way home
I'm sure
you found someone new

It's alright
I'll put on that slip dress,
you like
the red pumps
with the tie
I'll massage your scalp and twist
your locks
I'll play 'Round Midnight
while we make love
on the Futon
It's alright, baby

Just come on home;
I forgive you.

totally
for Iraq and Iran

Uh...yeah,
Like, I don't think,
they want a McDonald's or
a Wal-Mart

They're probably completely satisfied
with the 'nothing' we think they have

Uhm, I read the entire Constitution
I have never done this before
stopped at the first ten like Commandments
but this time...
Well, my mother was a pre-school teacher
and my father worked for
The VA making motivational speeches around the country
Ironic huh?
Well, he taught me how to memorize
So this didn't take long
but, like...
There was nowhere in the Bill of Rights that said we should:
take over other countries
impose our beliefs and government
or our God(s)
We learned the Pledge of Allegiance in Kindergarten
but, uh...I thought that was to our country and not just
the president

I'm sure the Middle Eastern accent would distort the words,
anyway and they aren't really trying to sing to our country tune
ya' know?

    But that's just my limited life

I mean ...
I remember when she stopped into my store
still in project:

Kill-An-Iraqui if those motherfuquers move, uniform
She was holding her hands up
spreading her fingers and frantically waving them in the air, like
she was trying to take off or something
her nails were still wet
and her weave, fresh from a new package,
was bouncing down her back
You could tell this was the expensive kind,
you couldn't even see the speed bumps in her head
When I asked her about it, she said she had reenlistment bonus
money to blow

She was coming to get a cell phone
These were her priorities:
Hair, nails, call loved ones
Pretty much in that order
and she told my co-worker and I this story
It was like that TV show where the girl witch snaps her fingers
and the world stops
and she gets to walk around in it until she is ready to
snap out of it again
'cause like, for a busy holiday weekend,
all of a sudden
no one came into our store until the
nail-blowing-weave soldier left

the bell over the door
was the only indication that she had walked out
and five people appeared at my counter with
their credit applications
bobbing in and out of line, peering over each other's shoulders
exaggerating the huff of their impatience
I was stuck on, like, stupid.

I'm paraphrasing, but, her story kinda' went something like:
She was out of the service,
her recruiter called and offered her $60k to reenlist
plus a $20k bonus for every year she signed up for
she became an MP

and her job was to kill anything moving,
including children
She came back to the states after her Tour and bought:
boobs
and a jag
and a house
pretty much in that order

I thought I heard someone on the news say, like,
this was a spiritual war
Like, when did we stop looking for God and start
looking for targets?

Hey ummm...I'm outside the President's self imposed 20 foot
Free Speech Zone,
Tab – which is funny because, I thought like the whole country
was a huge zone where you could speak freely, like uh,
in the 1st Amendment
Not the 2nd or the 14th but like number one, but hey,

That's my limited life

End tab.

So like,
I have a question:
Uh, did you all know that the 13th Amendment says:
Section 1. Neither slavery nor involuntary servitude, except as
a punishment for crime whereof the party shall have been duly
convicted, shall exist within the United States, or any place
subject to their jurisdiction.

This is the Abolition of Slavery Amendment,
so I was wondering, isn't making other people do what we
want them to do against their will, for the advancement of other
humans, like, involuntary servitude?
So my question is; since the President committed like 15,000
counts of murder, shouldn't his punishment be
slavery?

That's what that says right? "…except as a punishment for a crime…"

We could make, like, a citizens arrest and…do that
Impeachment thing-y
they tried to do to Clinton, for getting head in the oval office
That just made him…black

I mean, I know giving head on the regular makes my man
relax
that is why the whole country was doing so well
Clinton got some head
we were all at peace
no one was fighting…ok, maybe I'm getting ahead of myself
No pun intended
What about, like, the whole 8th Amendment: Excessive bail
shall not be required, nor excessive fines imposed, nor cruel
and unusual punishments inflicted
So, like the whole hanging thing, on American soil…
does the government miss the whole throwback, retro
punishment thing?

Didn't public mutilation, like, go out in the 60's?
Wasn't that left trailing behind pick up trucks?
with pieces of flesh left in the gravel for miles for hovering
vultures?
and blood left in the rope from wrists tied over their heads,
around broken ankles flopping behind them?
face singed from exhaust pipes
didn't cruel and unusual punishment drown
with the little girl bagged alive in a potato sack
and flung over a bridge
head smashed against the rocks
body torn to pieces by starving fish
left with so many holes in her face and chest her mother was
only
able to identify her
frail 11-year-old existence
by the yellow ribbon hanging loosely by sparse

strands of hair the:
men, potato sack, rocks, fish, sun, rain, wind and tide
couldn't rip out

Wasn't this whole civil war, racism thing drowned in that river?

That's just my limited life,
though

Speaking of war...Uh,
can we finally bring the troops home
like, totally?

No regrets.

Haiku for all wing clippers

If vulnerable
is where you want to keep me
take your clothes off, first.

dear God; it's me, sheba ...
however, you probably already knew that.

Faith = Dear God, I have no idea how to do this thing that I know I need to do but I'm sure you'll be around...laughing hysterically.

I'm about to make another huge decision; if we could leave out the acid reflux, this time, that'd be great.

P.S. Just because, I know you're a being of specifics and practical jokes, let me please add: indigestion ... heartburn (both kinds) ... doubt ... fear ... all that.

Thanks.

And not the THANKS, like I'm trying to be an ass or sound ungrateful, kind of "THANKS" (because we all know THANKS is intentionally rude and 99.98% of the time I'm looking down my nose or keyboard when I say "THANKS" to someone whether they know it or not.)

It's kinda' like when the British say "GOVNAH'"; they're not really being polite, they are being secretly condescending, which is what my usual "THANKS" means.

Not today.

Today, I mean "THANKS" like I know we're cool, kind of "THANKS". Like, you get me. You understand my swang. Not swag, swang. Like jive, dance moves with my words. Like the 20s meets the 50s doo-wop swang! We un-der-stand-each-oth-er-here.

Makes two fingered eye-to-eye "I see you" motion between self and sky

That kind of THANKS is today's THANKS.

I'll overlook you steering me through some seedy neighborhoods via Google Map just to remind me "where I came from" and "who I write for", which, if I could just TAB right here, God... Uh, if you remember correctly, not saying you wouldn't but you do have a habit of making things up as you go. (See your promise not to wipe out the earth AGAIN after the big flood, remember that?) Yeah, well ... If you remember correctly, (again, not implying ...) [Sigh/fake awkward cough to distract and move forward] you didn't really have me grow up or "come from" a seedy neighborhood.

We kinda' were OK for middle class teetering more toward too poor to really care 'cause my mother could sew and unbeknownst to our naive Americanized youthful selves, it was way cooler to have one-of-a-kinds than multiple manufactured over priced "fashion" off a mannequin in a store with neon signs inside a strip mall in which the only thing separating its name from their cousin's store a few blocks away is the name of any major city they think will attract urban youth to purchase sweat shop clothing where the screen printed picture of some animal, or the words: Sexy, Baby Girl, or Diva are written on the front will run if sweated in even a little too hard, leaving glitter embedded in the skin which will, undoubtedly, lead to a whoopin' 'cause yo' mama told you umpteen (Who made up that word, God? I mean besides you.

Who did you get to start the word "umpteen"? Had to be some old white woman. Was it? Was it my mama's mama? Or her mama? She was a German immigrant; did you confuse her speech one day after citizenship class and get my mama's, mama's, mama to start saying UMPTEEN? You can tell me; who was it? Can you point me in their direction so I can smack them right in the upper lip? You can't hide a swollen upper lip and I want everyone to know they made up a dumb-ass {Donkey, God ... you're the one that made double meanings for words. Why couldn't our language have stuck closer to Spanish?

We wouldn't be in half the mess we're in now.} word that has caught on generations later and now we're walking around saying things that didn't even make it into the slang dictionary.

Please tell me who started this and I'll call on a favor from my dead uncle on my father's side to slap them in the upper lip. Leave it all red, swollen and throbbing like a Fat Albert cartoon character. I mean you gone' be there to witness it so no need in lying.) times not to go outside in your "GOOD" clothes.

UNTAB: Back to you, God;

I'll forgive you for trying to scare the heeby-geebies (Who in the world started that one? They had to be African. Heeby-Geebies? That sounds like an African word. Word for ... for ... some sort of ritualistic dance.

Naw; I'm lying, it sounds like some distorted name for a disease. Like the origin of the word got lost in translation. I was lying out loud when I said "dance" but you already knew that... or did you? See that's what I don't get; I was still thinking "disease" but you let me go right ahead and say "dance".

If you KNEW I was thinking one thing and gonna' say the other AAAAND you "supposedly" [does quotation marks with hands] pre-write this whole thing, why don't you just script in all the right things to do?

Too much like right, huh? Nice.) Out of me. You know I drive solo, mostly. So I don't understand why you'd have Google Maps go in all sort of crazy directions, over railroad tracks through neighborhoods where their electric meter is preset from the regional {insert state here} office.

Again, I don't see why you just don't write in a direct route for me.

That's where I think SOMEBODY'S lying. Maybe not you, per se, but SOME-body is lying. You couldn't have pre-planned this whole life on earth thing AND offered up free will; that's a whole contradiction.

I still think you and Jesus and his 12 flunkies still exist (we won't get into how you can be three beings all at the same time, cause that would mean you were talking and praying AND SAVED yourself ... Which YOU invented this thing called schizophrenia to explain all that away {that was your escape clause wasn't it?!! WASN'T IT?!!! You, Che Guevara AND Nat Turner! Y'all were just schizophrenics in disguise as Jesus, Buddha and Allah...Nice. Nice one God. You're right no one saw that coming... We'll get into that later...)

I just think someone's been lying to us about why You slash Jesus slash the Holy Spirit needed to take a long weekend behind a rock. I mean, what? You needed a few days to reconsider this whole "Do as I say or burn for eternity" proposal? (And just an FYI that's not really a choice but since more people are following you on Twitter, Imma' let you have that. #imjustsayin) Which furthers my point on not making any sense whatsoever.

You can't tell us "it's all pre-planned and already written" if we get to choose. If it's all prewritten then we DO get to be mad at you, question, curse your name, throw rocks at the sky and trick you into letting R. Kelly, Woody Allen & Michael Jackson into Heaven; for all the natural disasters, disease and famine because you've admitted to premeditated murder and I've watched enough Law & Order to know we don't make deals on that one!

Deal or No Deal, God!?!

What's it gonna' be? Prewritten and blame you for it all and forget to praise you because we're too busy trying to figure out how to tie up your angels and make them watch reruns of The Brady Bunch?

Or — see if the banker has "Free will; the ability to choose our own paths without that whole burn forever clause" in one of the suitcases?

No switching-up the suitcases either! Let us get one right for a change.

You don't really want us walking on eggshells around you, now do you, God?

We're pretending to be good to our neighbors, while trying not to notice their grass is a little thicker than ours, stealing their lawnmower and tipping the neighborhood crack-head {the divorced dad on a teacher's salary that only gets supervised visits once a month with his two: young, impressionable, probably listens to mommy knock down daddy all day while the new boyfriend takes them to soccer practice in his new shiny sports car, children} to sell it back to the same neighbor to catch up on child support.

God, I'm sure you don't want the wrap on sabotaging our neighbor's cable box, outside, so they actually have to spend time talking to each other and not glued in front of one of their nine flat screens. (Not that I counted the empty boxes on their curb or anything) If you just fess up and admit it's all free will and you can't really make us do anything, which includes burning in hell!! Then we can't blame YOU for all the "natural" disease and disasters; we'll blame ourselves and praise you out of pure faith, not from you twisting our arm. You big bully!

Anyway...I just want you to know I got you. [Gives God fist bump and pounds chest twice with right fist] And I know ... I know ... Spread your Word ... The Gospel and all that. I'm on it. Imma' set up a automated Hootsuite account for you right now with daily Bible verses and all that! I'll add you on Facebook and after about 10 minutes the whole world will know your name; you know I'm famous (Thank you by the way) and as soon as I add you folk are so nosey (like Facebook isn't public. Do you know that someone tried to call me on commenting on something they said, even though they were having a conversation with someone else, in open forum? Silly me, of course you do.) they're gonna' wanna' know who I'm adding and shiiii ... My bad.

See that's what I'm talking about right there! You being who you say you are wouldn't have written in me cursing at you.

Come on! We all know you're too vain for that: "Me or the devil ... Me or the devil ...Me or the devil..." Seriously? Seriously, God? Listen to yourself, right now; you sound real immature. Not the business.

How you gonna' kick us down to Lucifer and you know how he is!! All possessive and controlling. He's responsible for the new VH1 show: The OCD Project. Plus, you kicked him out for trying to take your spot and if it was "already written" like you claim, [over exaggerates rolling neck and eyes] then you would've just killed him off abruptly & completely like Kutner's suicide on House. (Nobody saw that one coming.) Nice going FOX ... Er ... God.

Anyway, again ... I'll start a whole marketing campaign for you. I'll even secretly disguise your praise in borderline controversial love songs for my lover like Be Be & Ce Ce Winans... AND! I'll forgive you for malfunctioning my perfectly good, hot, GPS.

TAB: Which wasn't really hot; my friend gave it to me even though it wasn't hers to give. UNTAB. Although it didn't have the most updated roads and the Points of Interested were all old Wal-Marts along dirt roads, it talked me through rough places all around the southeastern region of this country (that I'm just gonna' go ahead and safetosay you did NOT tell Columbus to come over here, rape, kill, torture and sell us folk of color with his non-navigating ass. {sorry, again} I'm just gonna' bet that wasn't you. We'll blame it on FOX NEWS. Too many blondes.) and actually found the shortest routes without taking me around the damn (that's not a bad word; it's a beaver's house) world like you have Google Maps do to me; if you forgive me for:

Everything.

Love, Bethsheba (that, too, clearly was no coincidence) A. Rem

P.P.S.(remember, the P.S. was in the beginning) I don't know why I signed the letter IF you already wrote it; you should know who it's from.

My bad. Habit.

-She ... Shi ... Ugh.

my dichotomy

The Wise ones
once told me that
If you can
Deny
Indulgence
Gluttony
Promiscuity
the Same Sex
the privilege of race
the playing of god
hopelessness
Slavery
Evil
Abuse
Futility
burning bridges
Lies
temptations
Frigidness
Crime
pimps
hierarchies
Puppet Masters
Selling Out
Arrogance
And much more
But
Believe
The boy Dynamic
Rest for the ages
sleeping when you are dead
keeping your temple clean
that spirits, smoke and intercourse clear the mind
the many can sometimes decipher the papyrus of the mind
cunning linguistics
the power of children for revolutionary change

Responsibility
the Freedom of Love
Unity
to be Optimistic

to destroy the Pessimistic
Mental Evolution
the concept of an eye for and eye
a tooth for a tooth
last chances

Sobriety

the sanctity of Verbal Drums
Love conquers
that Hate can exist
the joy of two becoming one
Exploration
Perseverance

Dreams

loose lips sink Ego ships
friends should be kept close, enemies closer
Travels of the Mind
everyone should have their own castle
that the concept of the question "Why" makes me supreme

Movements

that with words spoken I can move mountains
armed struggle and the might of Pens
that most will die without everyone knowing they lived
that Businessmen should fund revolutions
the power of Urban Soldiers
War and Conflict

Resolution

Poets as Leaders
that those who know, should pave the way
in Liberation and Redemption Songs
that Life is based on Choices
in knowing that just knowing, is the key to everything
then
your dichotomy
shall be the truth
spoken
guiding the path
for those who
seek
themselves
in the mirrors

of existence.

Don't tell the world you're coming, just show up

the grass is not always green – er

you may be living on Astroturf and don't even know it

I think about people from my past. Randomly.

Let me back up.

Networking has got to be one of the most powerful tools in the world. I mean, think about it; even with the "oldest profession in the world" there had to be some networking to keep business going 'back in the day.'

One John had to tell another John about what a great time he had in the garden of Eden for that business to become the multi-billion-dollar industry that it is today; complete with porn dolls and MySpace.

I imagine that prostitution, then, was with women dressed in all white with flowers adorning their heads and men bringing them livestock, gold and entire cities for their time well spent. Not the sporadic trips to a three star hotel, restaurant with an all you can eat buffet and some Air Force Ones or a Gucci bag for the ones that look the other way, that we are so "privileged" with today.

Naw, I imagine our va-j-j's were worth a few cities and a couple dead gladiators "back then."

Networking is a beast. Don't knock who you meet. File them away if you have to but don't knock them out of the social ring. Thank you Kimberly Sharell; author, poet and Blog Talk Radio host for sending me Maya Simmons, my new attorney.

Mrs. Simmons (I'm sure she wouldn't mind being called Maya she is in my age bracket <30 but she deserves a level of respect putting white collar criminals and law benders … not behind bars … but under a pile of paper work and legal headache. Way more fun.) and my relationship started around Rough Language.

Yes, even poetry events have red tape. Tsk. Tsk. Tsk.

She came by the other day to drop off some paperwork and was having trouble finding my house inside my maze of a subdivision. Whoever designed it needs to burst into flames and turn in their engineering degrees.

I had just returned from the dog park. My not-so-favorite white pants were a tad dingy and I had grabbed any ole' shirt off the hanger to jump in the car and get out to get some sun.

This was about 3 hours ago. My shirt was a thrift store, or maybe swap meet, or hand-me-down from a friend, that was too big and I hadn't found it's magic just yet so it became my grab and go to somewhere I don't care what I look like shirt. It was tunic like. Hung over my pants a little and cut low in the front in a v. The yellow and blues mixed in some abstract pattern with the browns gave it a little life but I had already decided to keep it only to garden or run to CVS or, obviously, the dog park, in.

I was fashionably slumming. I was extremely comfortable.

Standing outside on my driveway, with my great Dane, Spirit, giving directions on my cell to Ms. Simmons, on the other line was my home-girl, Femcee and PhD candidate Khalilah Ali. I was flipping back and forth on my iPhone; giving directions to Ms. Simmons on one line and talking with Khalilah about finding and making a decision about a graduate program on the other line.

As I waited for Maya to find my house with the, yes, fourth – seemingly simple – set of directions, "Go straight, left, then around the circle, past the church, up a hill, 4th red door on the right … next to the fence with a peace symbol on it …"

I swapped lines and continued talking to Khalilah about her PhD program at Emory, "Yeah, man … I'm looking for an all inclusive program with a stipend and tuition scholarships…"

As I head toward the mailbox to relieve its throat of all the bills choking it out, and Spirit on my heels (as trained – no leash) my neighbor who lives immediately across the street from me, the young wife, and her two just adorable children (don't ask me their names) pull into their driveway.

The children spring out of the car doors, opening its ribs and spilling out of the sides of their average blue probably early 2000s Pathfinder. (Oh, I'm not judging, my car is almost 10 years old – this'll be important in a second – hang in there).

The girl, a few years older than her brother, long pony tails way past her shoulders, immediately heads for the street. She loves Spirit. Spirit loves children. (Most great Danes do. They have a keen temperament for little people.)

She flings her pink backpack over her shoulder with some Cartoon Network character on the front I can't make out in the blur, and heads for the end of her driveway.

The mother, who's name I can never recall, or I kind of think I remember but am not sure, laps the back of the SUV and notices me in the drive. "Hey!" She projects to get my attention, "We have on the same outfit!"

I glanced her way without responding and noticed the similarities. White pants, flat sandals and a tunic-like shirt that hung over the top of our pants but isn't quite flattering save the V-neck cut. Her shirt was shinier and had better color.

I remember thinking, "Uh, yeah but it's whack and you're excited you have it on."

All in that .2 seconds I thought about how boring her life must be. Her husband was average looking, she was nice enough but didn't seem real exciting or excited about much. The most fun they ever have at their house is their children's birthday parties.

Their yard is always a mess; there is one huge pink rose bush growing out of control covering their front window. All their shades are always drawn making it look dreary from the outside. There is this one curtain in an upstairs window that is bunched up on a ledge and I always try and imagine what's behind the curtain. I never see it move and the light is always on in that room.

I imagine it's an office, where she sews communion dresses for her daughter or helps her son with his science project or reads to them at night.

I only see her and her husband in passing. One night on my way out to a reading, they and their children were outside with a visiting friend and I told them the brownchickenbrowncow joke. They kinda giggled and I heard him say "No, Spoken Word, I think," under his breath as I got into my car and drove away to my exciting life in the night and left them standing on the curb of their boring, predictable life; regulated by school schedules and business meetings. So I thought. Or wished. Or imagined.

One night, insomnia was getting the best of me and I took Spirit to the front yard to play catch. The husband/father comes home 3-4am, in his little rusted, red, hatch back, turning the corner at the end of the block on two wheels, stereo blasting whatever was on the radio, muffled by factory speakers and rolled up windows, burns rubber turning in his driveway, stumbles out of the car and slams the door.

"Are you alright?" My normal tone of voice was magnified by the silence of the night.

Our neighborhood is normally quiet. We have two predators; bold robbers and a family of deer. Only one is nocturnal.

He looks dead at me, laughs a full laugh and wobbles in the house. Closes the door behind him without answering.

I imagined he was out cheating. I don't even know the man.

I discounted it almost as fast as I thought of it. First to give him credit and second because he'd never, in the years that I've lived there fighting insomnia on the front yard with Spirit and/ or jogging or riding my bike through the neighborhood at the witching hour, noticed him behave like that.

I then deduced he was stressed from work. Bored at his mid-life-realization and went out and got drunk with the fellas. Maybe the wife was out of town and it was his only chance to escape without having to explain, ask for permission or report his whereabouts.

Spirit and I looked at each other, shrugged and kept playing I throw the ball and you bounce around and go get it.

Another time, I remember the father/husband telling me his wife loves Ikea and that his "entire house" had that "Ikea crap" all over.

He said it with disgust. Like he was disappointed that their furniture or whatever "crap" he was referring to didn't come from a better store.

Ikea gets a bad rap for its inexpensive items but if pricey is what you're looking for they definitely have that, too.

I've always lived wide open. Shades open. Windows open. Heart open.

I understand why people always have their shades drawn, I just think if you invite the light in, darkness has no place to hide.

Ever since bored-husband told me about the Ikea "crap" it wasn't hard for my imagination to build Ikea coffee tables, futons with throws across the foot, stacks of useless Ikea glassware, plastic tubs, plastic organizing towers and millions of toys laying around their house.

My mind created every room an Ikea heap pile. Unable to sift through. Kind of like the Hoarders show but without the grime. For some reason I didn't picture dirt just piles of plastic "crap".

The flashback ends and I shout back, "I like your shirt way better!"

I take Spirit by the neck, and go to meet them in the middle of the street. The wife hears me talking to Khalilah about grad school.

"GA Tech has a great grad program, too..." she starts. I shoulder my phone to keep it from dropping and motion Spirit to sit so pig-tails can pet her. The little boy retreats behind the hissing Pathfinder, he and Spirit still see eye-to-eye and he's not comfortable, yet.

No worries; I found that if you don't force people to do what they don't want to, they tend to come around, eventually, anyway.

"Yeah, I know..." I say and pull the phone away from my ear realizing Maya had hung up and called back, probably getting frustrated by now. "I even found out Tech has a MFA in Creative Writing from an older poet that teaches there... I wouldn't have even found out if ... Hey Khalilah," addressing the phone again, "Let me call you right back."

We hang up and I'm standing for the first time face to face with the wife of some guy and their two children, who's names I can't recall, that have lived directly across the street, for almost three years, from me.

She started telling me about how she works in the marketing department at GA Tech. "I don't do anything creative ..." she stops to correct herself "... I mean, I'm a creative person (here we go, I thought) but my job isn't ... I work in the marketing department..."

"Oh." I said completely uninterested. Booorrrriiiiiiing. "That sounds cool," I was half lying. I think marketing is really cool actually but she didn't seem like she knew anything about 'real' marketing and what does a black woman who thinks a tunic is a 'cute outfit' know about marketing a major university? I'd loooooveeee to see what marketing plans she came up with.

Snide doesn't work so much when you keep it to yourself but it's cruel out loud. Either way you lose.

I was being an ass in my head.

Nice, Sheba. You don't even know this woman and you've already summed up her life. Or her lack of life.

Who the fuck are you? I'm yelling at myself, in my head now, totally staring through this random Erin woman, wife, mother. For some reason her name did stick; Erin. No it's not like that! I just remembered it. It probably was the easiest of all four of the family names.

It stuck with me.

I think about people from my past; randomly.

I don't think about random people from my past. I think about people, from my past; randomly. Specific people.

I think about our middle-school teacher Ms. What's-her-name that everyone hated but I got along with so well and wondered why that was so.

I think about my brothers that I never talk to. Someone was flirting with me the other day. Chatting me up and asked about my family. I couldn't tell them what my brothers did and/or where they were, geographically, in life. I have no idea. But I think of them.

I think about this other middle school girl that I mocked in front of our entire class, embarrassed her, basically made her look like a slut and then almost got my ass kicked later in the hallway.

Ha ha – as I remember it – she was charging toward me and a group of friends laughing and recounting the scene in the gym. She was a "popular" girl. Her light skin turned flashing stop light red. In and out of her cheeks; puffing up and sinking like a flat kick ball being inflated by a foot pump. She was pissed.

There was a rumble in the background of the changing classes and the last thing I heard was "No! No! It's not worth getting kicked out! School's almost over!"

Her then-friends were holding her back so tough, her butt was sliding across the hallway floor, her feet still kicking in the forward walking motion and one "friend" had each one of her arms by the wrist above her ears dragging her back down the hallway.... What was her damn name? She was a year older than us.

I wonder where kickball cheeks is and what she's doing. I wonder if she has any of those same "friends".

I think about my neighbor, a boy two years older than me, who molested me every day after school. I heard he moved to Atlanta to become a rapper in the early 90s. The game quickly gave him the boot and he returned home to Detroit. Right back next door, living with his mother and white stepfather. A teacher.

I returned home in '96 to take my son home to meet my mother. Dejected rapper happened to be home and had suffered a serious stroke, or something, and his face was distorted so badly that my 2-year-old son called him a monster to his face.

The irony.

I wonder if he is still alive.

I think of Carl Smith, who I had a serious grade school crush on and was so disappointed in him when he chose our middle school hood-rat to take on his very first date ever.

She came back and bragged about how he paid for the $5.00 (for two!) movies with a $20. Gold digger.
I see Carl on Facebook and wonder what his life is like but don't really want to know.

And ... I think of Erin Green, Joy Smith and Amanda Quick.

We were all light skin black girls with long hair. Although Amanda is white, she was also a "light skin" black girl. She wasn't the annoying white girl trying to be black, she was white – white but cool.

When her cup size went from training bra to 36D over the summer between 6th and 7th grade, it didn't matter what color Amanda was to the boys. She had boobs.

Amanda, Joy and Erin's parents had a little money. We all lived in the same neighborhood but while my parents were fashion misfits and believed the only time to go shopping was for the beginning of the school year, birthdays and Christmas (my birthday is 2 weeks before school started, so my shopping was limited to twice a year and I wasn't allowed to make up the budget difference in the summer), Amanda, Joy and Erin were always fly.

Nu – Nu in the movie "ATL" was Erin Green in my middle school. Always the freshest gear, she had thick naturally curly hair down her back and always sported a new sweater and penny loafers. Erin rocked the Nu-Nu. She, Amanda and Joy were joined at the hip.

I envied their clothes. When Amanda and Erin cut their hair to mirror the sweeping Prince trend, I asked my mother to cut my hair like theirs and she said, "Uh… you may be mixed but you don't have hair like theirs. It won't look the same." I ended up with the asymmetrical Salt-N-Peppa look.

Remember riding boots? Joy always had a fresh pair of riding boots. Every freakin' color. Or it seemed. Especially to an 11-year-old coveting child.

One day in the 6th grade Joy came to school with a fresh sweatshirt with a college name on the front, some skinny jeans that cut off at the ankle, white socks and some shiny loafers with a quarter in each one. Amanda looks her over and says, "What's wrong with you, today?" "I'm moving, remember?" Joy replies looking at the floor. "Oh yeah…I forgot. I was wondering why you were looking so bummy." Said Amanda and walks away.

I remember thinking, "What in the hell is Amanda talking about?!? Joy looks fresh as hell!!"

I'll never forget that.

I had to turn my clothes inside out to make it seem like different clothes as the school year progressed. I was always washing my sneakers and had to beg for another pair when the fresh white look would start to turn yellow with all the bleach in the wash.

I even dyed a few pairs I had in cloth.

I envied everything I thought their life was like. Especially Erin Green. She was the closest one of the dynamic trilogy I could relate to. We were the same color, height and same bushy hair ... well ... almost the same.

Erin was beautiful. I wanted to be her.

Her brother, Forest (yes, Forest Green) was fine as hell. He never looked my way.

I was mad at my parents for not being more trendy, hip and cool. We drove a mini van and my dad played softball in the summer, with his office. My mother wa... is a teacher. She taught me and my older brother in pre-school. She also draws and paints.

I wonder if she still does.

Pigtails was hugging Spirit tight around her neck, Spirit was panting and wagging her long tail; she was soaking up all this affection from a familiar little girl with new smells, and the wife of my neighbor who's lived directly across the street from me for three years, named 'Erin' and I were standing in the middle of the street.

"You look just like this girl I went to middle school with," random Erin says looking me dead in my face.

Because we were neighbors, we've introduced our families to each other several times but obviously neither one of us cared enough to remember. Even pigtails, who's brain should be an untainted sponge only remembers Spirit's name.

"Oh, yeah?" I say, looking at her for the first time ever.

"Where're you from?" I ask. "Detroit." She says.

"Really?!" I start to look her over. Graying smooth hair, cut above the neck.

"What high school did you go to?" I immediately recall her first name. Erin. I mean, I knew it was Erin but I started to question if maybe the little girl's name is Erin, or the father's name is Aaron.

"Cass Tech." My forehead starts to wrinkle and I squint my eyes tight like "What!?!"

"What year did you graduate," I ask almost hoping she doesn't say our year.

" '9…"

I didn't let her finish. (Well, I did but I'm not telling y'all what year I graduated high school!)

"Shut the fuck up!" I blurted out and immediately realized shy boy had emerged from behind the boring blue Pathfinder and managed to start petting Spirit's back without freaking out. We both looked down at the children. She made a loose failed attempt to cover their ears, which ended up being their eyes.

"I'm sorry," I said quickly.

Most of us ended up at Cass Tech, the famous school for the arts that mirrored its learning program after Fame in New York.

We lost each other inside high school. Our middle school was 1000 for all grades and Cass had a graduating class of 1000-1200. With over 4000 children in one school, we all formed new groups. I didn't stay at Cass long, anyway. Was shipped off to my first youth home in the middle of 10th grade.

The top three high schools in Detroit were/are: Cass Tech, Renaissance and MLK.

If you went to Cass you were nerdy, stuck up, and artsy. Those students most likely ended up being involved in the entertainment field, artists, visual artists, dancers, musicians and grassroots organizers.

If you went to Renaissance you were nerdy, a bookworm and had no life. This was our rival school. These students most likely ended up being professors, scientists, bio-chemists, astronauts and PhD candidates.

If you went to King you were nerdy with street smarts and some edge. These students most likely ended up being the slightly crooked attorney's for the Cass students.

We are Technicians. Well ... they were.

In February of our sophomore year, I was shipped off; without warning or major announcement to Wedgewood Acres. A youth home in Grand Rapids, MI, about 3 hours NW of Detroit.

I returned to Cass, briefly, in my junior year after a year at Wedgewood but then had to leave again to Grand Rapids due to some legal mumbo-jumbo about my adoption and being ward of the state and Wedgewood's open housing program. There were a lot of holes. Wait for the book.

I was traumatized the first time I had to leave my lifelong neighborhood "friends" in the 10th grade, then almost paralyzed when I had to leave the second time. It took a lot for me to return to Cass, there were rumors about what happened to me: I was in a crazy house, I had ran away, my 'real' parents came back for me, my adopted parents went nuts and killed everyone except me ... all sorts of chaos.

I won't even get in to how my track team at Cass was the shit. We were beginning to break records and some of us were trying out for the Olympics in '9 ... (yeah). When I couldn't run with Cass's program any more and joined a sorry ass team at Grand Rapids Central I lost speed and ambition.

A few of the Cass girls made the Olympics. I tried and didn't make it. I, technically, graduated high school from Grand Rapids Central but never claimed them. I was a Technician and always will be.

Rosedale Park for Life, sun! (Yes, I know I spelled it with an 'u'. I figured you all are too old to be called 'son' and it's a little disrespectful. I call you all 'sun' because I know you all have the ability to shine.)

I lost track of them all when I left Detroit the 2nd time. I didn't even try to find them. So I thought of them, randomly.

I figured I'd never see any of them again. And tried not to think about it.

When I graduated high school I had heard that a few of the girls in my class at Cass all went to Spelman College, in Atlanta.

I had decided to run wild in the streets. I had no home, no responsibilities and no one to be accountable to.

I bounced around for almost a year after high school and then moved to Norfolk, VA with a high school sweetheart.

We got married and annulled all in four months.

I liked Virginia. It was warmer than Michigan, it had a beach nearby and I always loved to swim and then I had no concerns about the economy so I found an apartment, rent-to-owned some expensive looking cheap furniture and got the current boyfriend to drive me wherever I wanted to go. Found a job at the 2nd busiest McDonald's in the world on the world's largest Naval base and partied for four years.

When most of the Technicians were graduating with their bachelors, I finally decided to settle down and attend Old Dominion University.

Graduated four years later, got fired from what I thought was the be all, end all to all jobs in the land at the monster we know today as Bank of America, which afforded me my first Acura, long sculptured acrylic nails every 2 weeks, child care for my 2-year-old, town house rent and club money.

I had even graduated to Express from Lerners and from DSW (which as an adult I know is the shit now) to Nine West and from fake Coach bags out of the fake Coach catalogs to a man (now experimenting with women) to actually buy me one.

This was my life.

You couldn't tell me shit.

Note to insecure poets, people that say/think I'm unapproachable – You're a limited thinker if you think I only started existing at my first poem. Which was, actually, in the second grade if you want to get down to it. But as we know it, college.

I thought I was the shit way before I was ever introduced to what we know as poetry/Spoken Word today. I was a survivor of many things I'm leaving out of this blog, turned short story, and for all the reasons in it. I have a story that starts lifetimes before I met you.

If you think I'm tough, I am.

If you think I'm a bitch, you're right ... for the wrong reasons.

If you think I'm unapproachable and mean, you haven't approached me.

End note.

1998 I came into consciousness.

2001 I cut my hair so I could take myself more seriously.

I wanted to see if I thought I was still beautiful without all the typical things that are supposed to make a woman "American male-textbook" beautiful.

I loved myself more.

I think about John Goode. I don't get to talk to him often. I think about the time I came to Atlanta with a singer and friend of mine Nina Ligeon, when we lived in Virginia. We stayed at his house. He let me borrow his clippers to tighten up my Caesar. I forgot to put the guard on and ended up cutting my hair to GI Jane length.

I remember walking down the stairs and he and Malik just stared. It got silent for 30 seconds. It felt like I was walking in slow motion and the sounds of laughter resembled fog horns right before the ship would hit the rocks.

John had gotten Nina and I a show at Soul Sista's Juke Joint at the Apache Café that night. We sang the shit out of our song, had one of the best performances of our lives. Standing ovation, tears, rocked the house.

I remember a sister name Phillippia was in the audience, mean as shit. Barely spoke to us. I thought she was f-n amazing. She sang Orange Moon and an original song and I wished to have 1/10th of the pipes and confidence she had, one day.

There was another group there: Slick & Rose. Another Atlanta favorite. They went up after us and I remember no one paying attention. I remembered them, though. They sang a new-then, now crowd favorite, song called "Milk and Honey".

I remember Kimmi, the founder of Soul Sister's Juke Joint, and how she took Nina and I to her house, made Nina and I some vegan food. It was so comfortable there I took off all my clothes and started walking around naked. Kimmi never lets me forget with her flirty ass.

I think about John because he is from Virginia and how I wanted us to be friends. I remember meeting him at my venue in Norfolk at the Jaffe Arts Center. I had just come off the road and had arrived late. They had already started and had booked John as the feature. I had heard of him and he had recently been on Def Poetry by then and wanted to check out his country twang story telling.

He was cool. Witty. Smooth. His poems rhymed. That was interesting to me. He handled his poems well. Didn't let them sound choppy and end-rhyme-y, like they could have if he wasn't sure about himself. He wore sweaters and jackets and his clothes fit. More interesting to me.

That was it. That's all I thought about him. It keeps replaying every now and again, when I recall those memories at his house in Atlanta, with his sister and Nina and Malik.

2001 – 2005 I traveled the world.

Had some magnificent accomplishments.

Had some significant tragedies.

2005 I moved to Stone Mountain, GA. Hated it. Wrote a roach poem about it and made my roommate cry.

I kept doing the poem. It is funny. Hilarious, actually.

She thought I was horrible for letting "the world" (like the world really reads my blogs or like "the world" all hears my poetry all at once) know we have roaches.

I said, "It's the south; everybody has roaches!" (I didn't add the 'just not as bad as we do in this hell hole,' part. I was grateful she opened her home to me in crisis. No one else did.)

2006 I moved in to the city of Atlanta.

2007 I bought my first home, ever. Had some panic attacks. Fought off normalcy. Warded off mundane.

Kept traveling. Kept running.

2010 I'm standing in the middle of the street, talking on my iPhone with an unlimited minutes and media plan, holding my great Dane by the choke chain for two young neighborhood children to pet her enormous gentle body, long ears, slobbery tongue and wagging tail, talking about grad school programs and giving my attorney directions to my home in the "city" limits but off the map. Literally.

Still traveling. Still running. Still making up shit to do. Creativity I think they call it.

"Erin Green!?!" I was totally freaking out by now. "You have a brother name Forest?!"

"Yeah – yeah" she starts nodding.

"Tell me your name, again" she was waving her hand in circles like it was on the tip of her tongue and she was trying to summon it by magic memory powers.

I got annoyed for a second. How could you forget me if you remember me? I let it go.

"Bethsheba!" I yelled it excitedly like we just met at the airport after being separated for years and we were just reunited by Montell Williams or Ricky Lake.

She repeats my name as if it'll help her recall all the memories she has of me. A whole two I'd presume. I'm underestimating my effect on people, again.

"Right ... right..." her voice fades while she searches her mental file cabinet. It must be a tall one.

"This is crazy! We've lived across the street from each other for almost three years!!? And we are JUST making this connection!?!"

They were posed like those question/statements. Most notable when someone wants you to do something for them: "You'll take me to the store?" Posed as a hidden question but the voice deliberately drops like a command or a statement instead of rising to give the receiver an option. There is no option. You end up going to the store if you wanted to or not.

"Shut up!" I started yelling. "Shut up!" over and over and over and over.

"Erin?! ... Erin Green!?!"

"Yeah!" She said smiling and getting a little excited.

"Get out of here!!!!" I repeat this at least 20 times, too.

"Oh my god! ... Yeah ... you ... Amanda Quick, Joy Smith, Carl Smith, Luandra Gardner, Francis Gruno...." I started naming half of our middle then to high school class.

"Wow," Erin says almost in disbelief. "You can name off everybody...I can't even ..."
She had to be lying, or hiding something. How can she not remember everybody!? I left and I remember the core.

Erin was there 'til the end, 'til the real graduation. Green and White gowns and caps, thousands of friends and family cheering on their accomplishments and crying over their futures inside Coba Hall or Joe Lewis Arena or somewhere historic to Detroit, not the Black and Gold 200 +/- children that barely made a 2.0 and graduated inside the gym with either no plans or their military recruiters waiting by the gym doors, dress blues and engine running.

Her voice was trailing off. I had started jogging down the street in my sandals holding Spirit by the collar to meet Ms. Simmons at the corner to lead her to my house, finally.

"I think about you!" I yelled over my shoulder. I started running backwards. "No, like I think about you- you!" I yelled. Immediately realizing that probably sounded really creepy.
I kept yelling a variation of sentences like:

"This is crazy!"

"I can't believe it"

"Erin Green?!??"

Middle school was purgatory; high school was hell. Both of them. Those idiots snubbed their noses and looked down their Trapper Keepers with glitter stickers on them to spell out their names so some flunky could return it to its rightful owner if they ever let their precious property out of sight.

We all used to sit in class with our pressed hair stretching down our backs. We'd sit with our necks all the way to the back to make our hair look longer than the girl next to us.

I'd get ridiculed for everything. Being bi-racial, adopted, smart. According to the middle school devils I was whiter than Amanda was.

I never made the top 10 cute girls in school list, none of the popular polls, and wasn't allowed out of my yard let alone the mall. At slumber parties I was the victim of falling asleep first pranks, which of course, gave me a complex as an adult, and was always egged on to take the "Dare" instead of truth. Either one was never supposed to leave the sleepovers. Yeah, right.

All my boyfriends were only on paper and I didn't even go to my senior prom. I did, however, go to my junior prom with the star basketball player.

He picked me up from youth home #2. I had to be "home" by midnight or I'd turn in to a Ward of the State. Nice.

When classmates from Cass (and Central) started to find me on Facebook I started to panic. I felt like they would know what I was thinking (like I'm not an open book), I felt like they'd only remember the ugly duckling and not recognize the swan.

Validation is key. They'd argue my crazy isn't artistic, it's always been there. I'm not sure if that helps or hurts me. That's funny. I just know I'm kinda' the same but better.

The same but sure.

Spring 2009 Stacey – I don't remember his last name – with big feet and held back two grades from our middle school, Ludington, arranged a meet up at a popular bar in a Detroit mall, when I happened to be visiting. I wanted to go. Sport my afro, tattoos, piercings and accomplishments. Look over their predictable lives and bask in my self assurance.

Look down my passport at them, wasting their lives in a dying city. Suffocating under the smog and unemployment.
I knew I'd be mad at them for not "getting out." For not leaving before the three children and high interest predatory lender interest rates on their mortgages drowned them. I wanted them to live off their dreams like I did. Build a backbone from the rubble of their mistakes and leave Detroit to crumble down on Kwame and the likes of him.

Arguing with myself again: "Who in the hell are you to determine one's happiness, Sheba? You're a bitch. How you gonna' act like you're so much better? Better than what? Shut up. Shut yourself up, right now."

I didn't go. I wanted to but I wasn't driving and my host wasn't really interested in hanging out with folk she had no connection with. To be honest, I was so nervous I might've barfed right on everybody's Sunday best. Or club gear.

I thought I'd see Erin there. I was hoping to see the trilogy there. Catch up, shoot the shit.

I imagined the scene in my head over and over. How I'd walk in. Who I'd gravitate to. My attitude. Light and fun or defensive and distant? Would I trip and look like an idiot? Get drunk and reveal my insecurities?

Up until standing in the middle of the street face to face with Erin Green, I regretted not pressing the issue more and getting over to the meet up. What opportunity would I have again to match up gators to stilettos, baby pictures, college stories and the who's married – single or married single and married and single, again, game.

I finally turned my back, stood at the end of my block and talked Ms. Simmons to my location.

As she turned down my street I let Spirit's choke chain go and raced her back to the driveway. She always lets me win.

Maya stayed long enough to drop off a contract she had been working on for me, wish me Happy Mothers day and drive off to her mini vacay for the weekend.

Erin, pigtails and shy boy had disappeared behind the rose bush, eaten by their front door into my imaginary abyss of Ikea clutter. I ran into the house past my dusty, neglected office, past the long empty kitchen with dishes in the sink, up the stairs that never get vacuumed, past the bamboo planter that never gets dusted, tripping over chew toys, collecting dog hair on the bottoms of my bare feet, left at the top of the cast iron stairs with wood banister that needs to be refinished, the loft that's in need of a 55"+ TV, a lamp, fan and another chair, through our master bedroom sparsely decorated with furniture from college, to tell my girlfriend of four years who I just decided last week I like,

that we have to move.

akoben

to the artist

This is still about freedom.
They will hunt you
leave gravel in your cheeks
scars across your forehead
brand your arms
and call you a club
a band of brothers
they will force guns
in your hands
and call you peace keepers
micro-chip your shoulder
and release you to the wolves.

Don't let these times confuse you
fool you
with black face
and white gloves
they will run their fingers
across your base boards
until they find fault
in your perfect
they will run you down
pull the plug on the sun
cut it off by the electric box
meter your usage
and charge you
for becoming too bright.

Hide your candles
in your socks,
learn to ignite flames
rocks and will, alone;
they will change the signs
on the road
leave blood dripping
through the mesh of the faucets

kept loose by land lords
as interest
holding your family hostage
like collateral damage
they will leave the blood
on the leaves to scare you.
Look up!
Don't let the limbs
fall on you
as you lean against the trunks
for rest.

They will ask you
to prove your poverty
on a dotted line
in triplicate
"Give me six references
that will vouch
for your misfortune."
Give them none
tell them God is too busy
working in places
he doesn't want to be.

Demand proof of life;
upload pictures of your children
on the playground in real time
they will anticipate your birth
pine box and serial number
you are an abortion
in reverse

Pull the trigger
when you're ready.

Life is like masturbation - Do you

untitled: haiku #27

unveiling bedrocks
worms, snakes, creatures wriggle out
build your path with stones

about the author
Books – Anthologies – Publications

- Nominated for NAACP Image Award for participation in the Check the Rhyme Anthology from Lit Noire Publishing, Nyc 2006
- Java Monkey Speaks Anthologies 2006-2010
- Creative Loafing Atlanta Guest Columnist October 2010
- 2007 National Poetry Feature for Rolling Out Magazine
- Essence Magazine
- Vibe Magazine Online
- Portfolio Weekly Magazine Cover Story
- Spoken Vizions Magazine Cover Story
- The Virginia-Pilot multiple appearances
- Recipient of the 2005 Virginia Fellowship for Individual Writer's Grant
- Awarded Book Serge book deal '05

forthcoming works

SOCIAL DISORDER
A play. Kinda. A one-woman show with other people in it. Sorta. An experience. For sure.

These are my F*#@-ing memories! Thanks.
Memoirs Vol.1–Memoirs & shit talking. Before the autobiography.

They Say
Alternative Rock Album. That's how "they" will have to box it in. It's really an album with music and words about speaking your mind, even if your voice shakes.[4]

RETRO ACTIVE® © 2010
You demanded it; you got it! The long awaited clothing line designed by Queen Sheba crafted by COTRICE © 2010 Fashions. A clothing line for funky fresh folk making moves. Just 'cause you're getting older, doesn't mean you have to look like it.

---

[4] A variation of a quote from an unknown speaker. "Speak your mind, even if your voice shakes." –Unknown